Domestic Airline Efficiency

An Application of Linear Programming

THE REGIONAL SCIENCE STUDIES SERIES

edited by Walter Isard

1

Location and Space-Economy
by Walter Isard

2

The Location of the Synthetic-Fiber Industry
by Joseph Airov

3

Industrial Complex Analysis and Regional Development
by Walter Isard, Eugene W. Schooler, and Thomas Vietorisz

4

Methods of Regional Analysis
by Walter Isard

5

Domestic Airline Efficiency
by Ronald E. Miller

Domestic Airline Efficiency

An Application of Linear Programming

Ronald E. Miller

The M.I.T. Press

Cambridge, Massachusetts

1963

Library of Congress Catalog Card Number: 63-10882
Printed in the United States of America

To my parents

Foreword

Dr. Miller's investigation of the airline industry is the fifth in the regional science studies series. It represents a case study of a basic component of the transportation-communications sector of a system of regions. Because basic linkages of a system of regions are reflected in and effected through the transportation-communications network, any penetrating study of a basic component of this network must of necessity be of interest to regional scientists and all others concerned with the study of spatial phenomena.

Dr. Miller's study has still further significance for the field of regional science. It represents an application of one of the most promising techniques in the field, namely, multiregional linear programming. Although the study does not consider locations as variables (that is, locations are taken as given), it does transcend the boundaries of customary linear programming analysis. It does utilize interregional flow data for an operating transportation industry. It establishes a norm against which to evaluate existing practices in this industry. It proceeds further and suggests optimal future interregional scheduling of aircraft flights under various assumptions regarding the state of technology (primarily as reflected in types of aircraft equipment). As a by-product of these projective models, insight is gained into desirable equipment purchasing policies by the airline industry. Finally, valuable materials are developed by which to appraise the effectiveness and adequacy of government regulation of this key industry within the U.S. system of regions.

For these reasons and others, Dr. Miller's study represents a valuable addition to the regional science studies series.

WALTER ISARD

Preface

This study takes inspiration from two sources. The first is the general development of mathematical frameworks in economics and regional science, especially linear programming methods, which has provided an ever-widening theoretical base from which to attack a broad range of problems. The second is the increasing interest in and concern about the domestic trunk airlines in the United States. Basic troubles in this industry have been highlighted recently by the introduction of jet-powered aircraft; the real causes go much more deeply and have been present since the end of the Second World War. It was with the hope of achieving some sort of reasonable balance between theory and application that this work was undertaken. Beginning with what is hopefully the firm foundation of mathematical programming theory, a structure has been constructed that is designed to provide at least some answers to a set of questions for which there may be many solutions. The method would seem to be applicable to a relatively broad range of problems; if such is the case, then perhaps the current volume will help to indicate a logical direction for future studies.

The present work has grown out of a doctoral dissertation presented to the Department of Economics, Princeton University, in May of 1961. Financial support for the academic years 1959–1961, during which this study was completed in its initial form, was provided by the National Science Foundation. It was then and has since been influenced by many people. A very basic debt must be acknowledged to Professors Robert E. Kuenne and Arnold Zellner, who, through their teaching excellence, are largely responsible for my conversion to economics in general and mathematical economics in particular. For constant encouragement, enthusiasm, and willingness to be of assistance at all times during the many phases of this study, I am and remain deeply grateful to Professor Richard E. Quandt. At an early stage, I profited greatly from discussions with Professor Richard E. Caves and Mr. Thomas F. Comick. I also gained much from the numerous and helpful comments of Professors Harold Kuhn and Oskar Morgenstern, as well as from a graduate-faculty seminar at Princeton University conducted jointly by Professors William J. Baumol, Fritz Machlup, and Richard E. Quandt. For their magnificent patience and knowledge of large-scale computing machinery, I owe thanks to Professor Foreman Acton, Dr. Herman Karremann, and the staff at the Institute for Defense Analyses, particularly Mr. John Harrell. Later drafts of this study were thoroughly read by Professors Jesse Markham, Benjamin Stevens, and Walter Isard, all of whom made many suggestions which corrected basic faults. Whatever clarity of exposition may be present is largely the result of the red-pencil reading done by Professor Isard and Mr. Murl Barker. Permission to quote was kindly granted by Richard D. Irwin, Inc., and United Research Incorporated. A final debt of gratitude is due Mrs. Madelaine Garber, who had the extraordinary courage to type the entire manuscript twice. I gratefully share any credits with all those mentioned above; criticisms I must bear myself.

R. E. MILLER

Philadelphia, Pennsylvania
December, 1962

Contents

List of Tables

Domestic Airline Efficiency

An Application of Linear Programming

Chapter I

Introduction

DURING THE LAST FEW DECADES there have been, among others, two important and complementary developments within the fields of economics and regional science, without which this study would not have been possible. One is an increased awareness of the importance of careful and regular collection of economic data on both a national and a regional basis. Largely through the efforts of government agencies and private organizations, an increasingly orderly wealth of statistical material is now more generally available to the interested researcher. The second characteristic which deserves particular mention is the development of sophisticated and complex mathematical methods, often grounded in elaborate abstract theory, which are of extreme relevance to economic and regional questions. These techniques provide more powerful tools of analysis that permit both reexaminations of basic problems in economic theory and also solutions to particular questions where previously only qualitative answers were possible. Linear programming is an outstanding example of such mathematical methods. Around it a large number of specialized techniques have grown up to deal with numerous well-defined particular problems. In the case of older questions, the results of reanalysis by more modern means serve either to confirm or to cast serious doubt on already existing notions. In either event, the conclusions are of as much interest here as they are when basically new or previously unapproachable problems are reexamined by means of modern programming techniques.

The present study makes use of linear programming theory as a guide to the construction of a model designed to represent a real-world situation. As such, it thereby becomes part of a general class of studies that are especially vulnerable to a particular criticism; namely, that the models employed are not adequate representations of the actual situation. This type of comment occurs frequently in current economic and regional writing. The philosophy upon which the present study is based takes a more optimistic view. Usually, the more complex the abstract model, the more accurately will it represent the real situation involved. However, a general consequence is that the more sophisticated a model becomes, the less workable it is, i.e., the chances are less that quantitative results are obtainable. This is not a happy consequence, inasmuch as such models are constructed in order that specific action can be taken on the basis of the particular solution values which result. One is continually aware of the problem of balance between realism and workability. A more relevant and constructive way to approach this problem of balance is to note, when analyzing the results of any particular model, to what extent any unexpected or especially surprising results are the direct consequence of particular assumptions involved, and further, if possible, how the outcome would be affected by relaxing these crucial assumptions.

This study is concerned with air transportation. An attempt has been made to isolate the salient features of the domestic trunkline system and to describe them within the format of a linear programming model. This is therefore somewhat related to that general class of linear programs known as the Transportation Problem, and it also resembles network flow models and interregional linear programming formulations in many ways. It is rather complex in structure but nonetheless can be represented in a reasonably simple set of relationships.

The optimal results of such a model — in the present case these are flights of aircraft between cities — can be put to many uses. In the present study, attention is centered on certain aspects of government regulation of domestic air carriers as effected by the Civil Aeronautics Board.[1] In particular, it is felt that new light is shed on at least one long-standing objective of governmental regulatory policy in the domestic air transport system: namely, on the concept of the efficiency of that system. One of the stated aims of government regulation in domestic air transportation is to provide the public with an efficient

[1] The term Civil Aeronautics Board will be used throughout this study to designate also that body which functioned as the Civil Aeronautics Authority from September, 1939, through June, 1940. The abbreviations CAB and Board will also be employed.

system. It will be argued later that neither in the detailed discussions carried on in economic cases nor in the resulting opinions and orders can one see a clear appreciation of the meaning of efficiency in this context. Further, it will be suggested that when the problem is described within the linear programming format outlined in this study, one of the outcomes is a set of solution values which describe an efficient system. These concrete results could serve as guides to pending and future cases before the Board. They also establish a standard by means of which it would be possible to make either temporal or spatial comparisons, i.e., to compare particular periods in the past or regions within the entire domestic system.

If such a method were employed, periodic review of the entire domestic system, as represented by the largest, most important traffic centers, would be possible. Regional studies could also be undertaken. On a smaller scale, the results of the analysis indicate to the CAB one measure of dollar costs that are associated with flight overscheduling.

It might be argued that it is not legitimate to select one individual aim from the entire set of CAB goals — the efficiency of the system — and give it such exclusive treatment. It is not difficult, however, to suggest other uses to which such an analysis might be put. These uses also provide justification for the development of the model and examination of the results. The formulation, for example, could serve as a guideline for similar studies of a number of other industries or of transportation systems of either larger or more modest scope. It could act as a supplement to other types of analysis in industry studies where "structure vs. performance" is at issue.

Air safety problems have become increasingly acute with the growing numbers of aircraft in the skies, especially as planes tend to cluster over large traffic centers. A complete record of the extra number of flights dispatched between any two nodes in the system is one of the results of the models used in this study. These and similarly derived figures for other sets of data provide a logical guide to investigators who might be interested in decreasing the aggregate number of aircraft in the skies in a way which would cause as little inconvenience as possible to the traveling public.

Moreover, individual airlines may be concerned with decreasing their costs whenever and wherever feasible. Such an analysis by a single airline would indicate the optimal number of flights necessary over each route segment in the entire system, i.e., that number which meets total demand at least possible total operating cost. It also is useful as a planning device, particularly with regard to equipment ordering policies that must anticipate needs by several years.

Finally, a by-product of the formulation in linear programming terms is a set of prices — the ideal rates that passengers would be charged if the industry were a purely competitive one. These might provide a new or supplementary yardstick against which the CAB could measure existing rates or proposed increases. A theoretically sound standard of reasonableness might be established, above which fares would not be allowed to rise.

The present study contains both theoretical and empirical sections. Chapter 2 is a résumé of the economics of air transportation. An examination of the nature of airline costs is important to establish a sound basis for the choice of cost data to be used in application of the model and also for a discussion of probable performance in the absence of government regulation. Demand characteristics, in turn, are relevant for that part of the analysis in which demand figures are derived for a time period in the future. Chapter 3 provides further background on which the rest of the study is projected, including a summary of the legal framework within which the Civil Aeronautics Board operates. It also contains an examination of certain historical cases and decisions that point out the lack of a consistent interpretation of efficiency and its meaning in the domestic air transportation system.

The two chapters in which the basic model is formulated and interpreted follow next. Chapter 4 presents the rationale for the use of mathematical programming models in studies of efficiency in an industry. This is followed by the model itself, including possible expansions and extensions depending on the ultimate use of the results. Further emphasis is put on an integer or discrete programming formulation and its relation to the inclusion of transshipment possibilities. The particular items in the general model of Chapter 4 are treated more fully in Chapter 5. Data sources are discussed as well as the technique of demand forecasting which was used for the projective model. Finally, there is a treatment of possible errors in models of the sort utilized in this study. Chapter 6 contains an analysis of the values that result from applying the model to particular questions, and conclusions are presented on the basis of these results.

Two years were selected for which the model was actually outfitted with data and solved. One was in the past, the other in the future. In order that actual historical allocation under the then-existing CAB decisions could be compared with the ideal results as defined within the framework of the theoretical models, a year in the recent past was selected. Specifically, 1957 was used because it was the last year in which predominantly nonjet service was available on long-haul, high-density routes. Therefore, certain comparisons between jet and piston service were also possible, since the results for a future year would be based on exclusive use of jet aircraft. Moreover, at the time this study was undertaken, 1957 was the last year for which the necessary data were available in complete form. The second year used — the one in the future — was 1963. It has been assumed that then all the routes considered will be served by jet aircraft, and a six-year projection from the complete data available up to and including 1957 seemed not unreasonable. The results of the 1963 model provide material for comparison of over-all economies of piston and jet aircraft. In addition, they indicate the optimal number of flight schedules over given routes under projected demand conditions and thus establish "target values" as a guide to long-range planning.

In each year, two formulations were used. The intercity model is concerned with traffic between particular individual cities. The inter-regional model, by contrast, treats geographical areas as aggregate nodes. All traffic is assumed to be concentrated at a city within the region, and the model is able to cover the entire domestic land area more fully, at the expense of less refined detail within the aggregate nodes themselves. It was necessary to treat the larger problem in this composite way because of an operational consideration. Modern computers were used for all the problems in this study. Without them the solutions to the particular problems would have been extremely time-consuming if indeed not entirely impossible. Computers, however, are necessarily limited with respect to the dimensions of the problems that they can handle. The number of nodes turns out to be the crucial factor in the case of the models formulated in this study. For that reason, wider geographical coverage was possible only through consolidation of cities.

It is significant that since this project was completed both increases in computer size and improvements in calculation methods for large-scale linear programming problems have impressively enlarged the dimensions of what constitutes a workable model. This knowledge was not available early enough to be utilized in the present study. It means that larger problems can now be analyzed with the models suggested here, thus contributing to the reality of the theoretical representation without decreasing the possibility of obtaining quantitative results. Such technological developments are very encouraging. They enlarge the possible scope of studies patterned after the one developed here. In a larger sense, they complement both the increasing availability of statistical data and the increasing integration of mathematical methods into economics and regional science.

Chapter 2

The Economics of Air Transportation

THIS CHAPTER serves as an introductory discussion of the general economic climate within which the domestic trunklines operate.[1] Occasionally, growth trends of the entire domestic commercial air transport industry will be noted. Insofar as trunklines are a significant proportion of this consolidated group, such figures will be meaningful for the more particular interests of this study.[2] In Section 1 the character of airline costs is discussed. The nature of demand and revenue sources occupies Section 2, and in Section 3 the relationships between market structure and market performance are investigated, with particular emphasis on probable behavior of the industry under complete government control and also under its complete absence. Section 4 serves as a summary.

It seems not inappropriate at this point to highlight the growth of commercial air transportation in this country. Numerous existing works contain an adequate description of the technological history and growth of the domestic air transport industry.[3] Some of this growth is indicated in Table 2-1, which compares service available in the

[1] This study is concerned with domestic trunklines. The twelve largest carriers with permanent operating rights, most of which operate high-density traffic routes between the principal traffic centers of the United States, are included. The airlines are the following: American, Braniff, Capital, Continental, Delta, Eastern, National, Northeast, Northwest, Trans World, United, and Western. United and Capital merged in 1961.

[2] Trunklines handle approximately 95 per cent of the total domestic air passenger-miles.

[3] The reader is referred to relevant sections of John H. Frederick, *Commercial Air Transportation* (4th ed.; Homewood: Richard D. Irwin, Inc., 1955); Thomas Wolfe, *Air Transportation Traffic and Management* (New York: McGraw-Hill Book Company, Inc., 1950); G. Lloyd Wilson and L. A. Bryan, *Air Transportation* (New York: Prentice-Hall, Inc., 1949); Joseph L. Nicholson, *Air Transportation Management* (New York: John Wiley & Sons, Inc., 1951).

United States in 1939, the year following passage of the Civil Aeronautics Act, with that in 1949 and in 1959.[4]

TABLE 2-1. GROWTH OF AIR TRANSPORTATION

	1939	1949	1959
Cities Served	286	638	721
Aircraft in Service	347	1,083	1,908
Daily Seats Available	5,100	35,900	109,710
Cruising Speed, Fastest Aircraft (mph)	220	315	615
Employees	13,300	76,000	162,029
Passengers Flown	1,864,000	16,723,000	55,875,000
Revenue Passenger-Miles Flown	728,900,000	8,827,400,000	36,300,000,000

Table 2-2 brings into sharp focus the growing role of air travel in the total domestic travel market. Commercial air transportation has not only grown considerably since its beginnings, as one would expect, but it has come to command an increasingly important share of the total domestic travel market. Table 2-3 presents the growth record of three measures of domestic trunkline activity.

TABLE 2-3. DOMESTIC TRUNKLINE GROWTH

Year	Passengers (000)	Revenue Passenger-Miles (000,000)	Passenger Revenues ($000)
1946	11,890	5,903	272,573
1947	12,279	6,016	303,194
1948	12,324	5,822	334,736
1949	14,021	6,571	378,113
1950	15,978	7,766	430,098
1951	20,621	10,211	570,288
1952	22,759	12,121	671,257
1953	26,137	14,298	775,782
1954	29,526	16,246	872,834
1955	34,511	19,217	1,021,855
1956	37,598	21,643	1,142,197
1957	40,270	24,500	1,287,172
1958	39,513	24,436	1,362,992
1959	44,488	28,127	1,632,646
1960	45,199	29,233	1,756,439

Sources: 1946–1953 figures from Air Transportation Association, p. 14 of Exhibit ATA-30, in *General Passenger Fare Investigation*, CAB Docket 8008.
1954–1958 figures from *Aviation Week*, May 4, 1959, pp. 93–124.
1959–1960 figures from *Aviation Week*, May 1, 1961, pp. 82–98.

[4] Figures for 1939 and 1949 from *Aviation Week*, May 4, 1959 ("Air Transport Facts and Figures" issue), pp. 100 and 106; those for 1959 from *Aviation Week*, May 2, 1960, p. 88.

TABLE 2-2. DOMESTIC INTERCITY PASSENGER TRAVEL
(In millions of passenger-miles)

Year	Railroad			Air*			Bus	Auto-mobile	Totals		Percentages				
	First-Class	Coach	Total	First-Class	Coach	Total			Common Carrier	All	Total Air to Total Travel	Total Air to Total Common Carrier	Total Air to Total Rail-road	First-Class Air to First-Class Rail	Coach Air to Coach Rail
1939	7,527	11,180	18,707	654	—	654	9,100	234,700	28,461	263,161	0.2	2.3	3.5	8.7	—
1947	12,261	27,665	39,926	6,063	—	6,063	23,948	272,958	69,937	342,895	1.8	8.7	15.2	49.4	—
1950	9,338	17,443	26,781	6,898	1,056	7,954	21,254	402,843	55,989	458,832	1.7	14.2	29.7	73.9	6.1
1952	9,504	19,758	29,262	10,105	2,356	12,461	21,223	495,547	62,946	558,493	2.2	19.8	42.6	106.3	11.9
1954	6,850	17,687	24,537	11,375	5,321	16,696	16,934	548,763	58,167	606,930	2.8	28.7	68.0	166.1	30.1
1956	6,275	17,074	23,349	14,204	8,074	22,278	16,409	617,713	62,036	679,749	3.3	35.9	95.4	226.4	47.2
1958	4,249	14,225	18,474	15,185	10,076	25,261	15,083	663,700	58,818	722,518	3.5	42.9	136.7	357.4	70.8
1960	3,650	13,200	16,850	15,957	14,418	30,375	14,400	660,000	61,625	721,625	4.2	49.3	180.3	437.2	109.2

* Domestic trunklines and local service carriers.

Sources: 1939 figures from *Aviation Week*, May 4, 1959, p. 119.
1947 through 1958 adapted from U.S., Federal Aviation Agency, *Statistical Handbook of Aviation, 1959* (Washington, D. C.: U.S. Government Printing Office, 1960), p. 80.
1960 from *Aviation Week*, May 1, 1961, p. 95. All figures, except those for air travel, are estimates.

1. The Nature of Airline Costs

For two specific reasons it is of interest to examine briefly the nature of costs incurred in domestic trunkline operations. In the first place, it is important to be clear on what cost elements are included in the parameters of the objective function in the linear programming formulation that will be the basis of the final parts of this study. When an objective of minimum direct operating costs is suggested, it is necessary to know what this means in terms of the air transport industry. Second, an investigation of costs, especially in relation to certain market variables and airline characteristics, should help to indicate whether or not there appear to be any scale economies in this industry. These results, in turn, will be germane to the speculations (in Section 3, of this chapter) on the probable behavior of firms if regulation were removed.

The distribution of total airline expenses is illustrated by the general expense breakdown in Table 2-4, and also by Table 2-5, which shows a more detailed division of expenses by the functional classes established by the Civil Aeronautics Board.

TABLE 2-4. GENERAL AIRLINE EXPENSES
(Per cent of total)

Employees	44.1	Promotion and Advertising	2.8
Supplies and Services	18.7	Taxes (not payroll)	3.2
Fuel and Oil	14.5	Interest	1.3
Depreciation	9.6	Other Expenses	1.7
Food	2.5	Profit	1.6

Source: *Aviation Week*, May 4, 1959, p. 98.

With reference especially to Table 2-5, it is clear that fixed charges are a relatively low proportion of total costs in the domestic airline industry. The figures do not seem to bear out the contention that the high-priced modern aircraft tend to make air transport an industry with high capital costs. This position is in contrast to the railroads, for example, largely because the higher speed of modern aircraft works to decrease the amount of capital equipment necessary per unit of output — the passenger-mile or the ton-mile. In addition, the fact that airways are maintained by the federal government and that airport facilities are supplied in large part at low cost by government agencies contrasts airline operations with the railroads. Airport services, to a large extent, are purchased as they are needed and thus

TABLE 2-5. DISTRIBUTION OF TOTAL OPERATING EXPENSES BY CAB FUNCTIONAL CLASS: DOMESTIC TRUNKLINES, 1956

(Percentages)

DIRECT EXPENSES 50.8		INDIRECT EXPENSES 49.2			
Flying Operations	*29.3*	*Ground Operations*	*13.2*	*Advertising and Publicity*	*3.0*
Crew Salaries	9.7	Ground Service Employees	5.8	Advertising Space	1.7
Fuel and Oil	16.9	Other Salaries	4.2	Other	1.3
Other	2.7	Other	3.2		
Direct Maintenance	*13.4*	*Ground and Indirect Maintenance*	*7.1*	*General and Administrative*	*6.9*
Labor	5.5	Salaries	5.7	Salaries	2.6
Materials	7.0	Other	1.4	Employees Welfare Insurance	2.0
Others	0.9			Payroll Taxes	0.9
				Other	1.4
Depreciation	*8.1*	*Passenger Service*	*7.2*	*Ground Equipment Depreciation*	*1.1*
Airframe	5.4	Cabin Attendants	1.6		
Engine	1.3	Other Salaries	0.6		
Other	1.4	Passenger Food Service	2.7		
		Other	2.3		
		Traffic and Sales	*10.7*		
		Ticketing and Reservations Salaries	5.1		
		Other Salaries	2.2		
		Other	3.4		

Source: Adapted from Air Transport Association, p. 11 of Exhibit 10D, *General Passenger Fare Investigation*, CAB Docket 8008.

become a variable rather than a fixed cost.[5] However, it does remain true that the addition of another passenger (up to the capacity of the aircraft) generally means little increase in airplane operating costs. Fuel, food service, and certain station expenses will increase somewhat. With the addition of another flight, total operating costs will rise, but all other constant costs will not increase proportionally, and average cost may decline.

Table 2-5 also indicates the presence of a high proportion of "indirect expenses" — costs associated with sales and passenger service as well as general ground operations. These may be caused largely by the technology of the industry, which seems to require an elaborate system of base operations and also provides a strong incentive to achieve as high an equipment load factor and utilization as possible.[6] These latter items, in turn, lead to relatively expensive reservation methods and services.[7] High sales costs are also attributable to the strong element of service rivalry among carriers. All of these factors imply at least some scale economies in the operation of the airlines.

The small domestic trunklines show substantially higher costs than the medium- and large-sized trunks.[8] However, at the other end, the large-sized airlines do not show very great cost advantages over the

[5] There is a frequently noted disposition in other forms of transport toward decreasing total unit costs as the important constant cost elements are divided among more units of output. Thus, increases in volume of traffic occupy a dominant role in planning, and introduction of price decreases is one way in which carriers might attempt to bring about such increases. This tendency is not as important in air transport. (It is, in any case, a relatively short-run idea; the same number of miles of track or airport buildings can accommodate increased amounts of traffic with only slight additional costs, up to some finite capacity limit.)

A distinction should be drawn between constant and fixed costs; the latter, such as some salaries or depreciation charges, would continue whether the airline operated flights or not, while the former are those costs that do not increase in proportion to output yet would cease if an airline suspended flight operations. These would include many airport (passenger handling) expenses and a large part of the payments to supervisory, clerical, and administrative personnel.

[6] Cf. John Meyer, M. J. Peck, John Stenason, and Charles Zwick, *The Economics of Competition in the Transportation Industries* (Cambridge: Harvard University Press, 1959), pp. 135–139.

[7] For example, TWA uses a $6.5 million reservation system involving high-speed computers. Reported in *The New York Times*, October 17, 1961, p. 78.

[8] Cf. Paul W. Cherington, *Airline Price Policy: A Study of Domestic Airline Passenger Fares* (Boston: Harvard University, Graduate School of Business Administration 1958), pp. 42–66, for an excellent discussion of scale economies in domestic trunkline operations. This is also discussed in Meyer *et al.*, *loc. cit.*, and Stephen Wheatcroft, *The Economics of European Air Transport* (Manchester: The University Press, 1956).

medium-sized carriers.[9] In his extensive analysis, Cherington finds differences in operating costs per available ton-mile and per revenue ton-mile between the "Big Four" trunklines (American, Eastern, Trans World, and United), the middle-sized (Capital, Delta, Braniff, Northwest, National, and Western), and the small carriers (Continental, Northeast). The differences between small- and medium-sized carriers, however, are much more striking than those between medium and large airlines. A very important factor favoring the large carriers seems to be their ability to concentrate the bulk of their operations on four-engine equipment, which Cherington shows to be inherently more economical in terms of operating costs per unit of output. The figures support his general conclusion that "the principal determinant of airline costs appears to be length of haul [passengers] coupled with sufficient volume of traffic to permit a relatively long average length of hop [aircraft]."[10] A second factor, of slightly less importance, seems to have been the introduction of large-scale methods in the equipment maintenance function.

The first item, the role of high-density traffic, is by no means a *consequence* of large-scale operations. However, it is one of the main advantages that the larger United States trunklines have over their smaller rivals.[11] Note, however, that since the large-scale operators have this density advantage, it is all the more significant that the overall cost picture indicates a lack of economies beyond the scale of operations of the medium-sized carrier.[12] One explanation would be that with further increases in scale of operation there is an attendant increase in unit costs (of management, for example) or diseconomy of scale. That is, the demonstration of the existence of certain economies of scale is not in itself enough to prove that the larger airlines will necessarily be more efficient than the smaller ones, i.e., will produce under conditions of lower unit costs. There remains the possibility that the large airline may suffer diseconomies of scale.

[9] Wheatcroft sets the point of division between large and medium carriers at about 150 million capacity ton-miles per year, *ibid.*, p. 78. The market was broken down as follows in 1959: Big Four (American, Eastern, United, Trans World) — 68.3 per cent of trunkline passenger miles; Middle Five (Braniff, Capital, Delta, National, Northwest) — 24.2 per cent; Little Three (Continental, Northeast, Western) — 7.5 per cent. Source: U.S., Civil Aeronautics Board, *Monthly Report of Air Carrier Traffic Statistics*, November, 1959, pp. 25, 29–31.

[10] Cherington, *op. cit.*, p. 50. Most of his data were for 1956.

[11] See footnote 41, p. 25.

[12] Cf. Wheatcroft, *op. cit.*, pp. 92–93.

There is also a second possibility. The smaller airlines may be able to reap some of the advantages of larger-scale operation through subcontracting certain functions to specialized firms. In a sense, this becomes the best of both worlds, for the economies of larger operation are not accompanied by the possible diseconomies. Especially with regard to overhaul and maintenance, some of the smaller airlines may find such avenues open to them.[13]

It is also not necessarily the case that demonstrating the probable existence of diseconomies after a certain firm size automatically ensures that the net effect will be an upturn of the cost function. It might happen that the increasing management and administrative costs were just offset by the continued economies of larger operation. In air transport the tendency seems to be toward a balancing of the positive and negative cost items. At least the economies do not continue indefinitely as size increases. This result will be of importance later in the discussion of various alternatives to regulation.

2. The Nature of Airline Revenue and Demand

Revenue

Airlines derive revenue from three major sources: passengers, United States mail, and express and freight. The distributions of these amounts are shown for the postwar period in Table 2-6. The predominance of passenger revenues is clear. For this reason the discussion of the fluctuations of passenger traffic and passenger demand will be taken as indicative of fluctuations in airline revenue in general.

Until very recently, the most prevalent view of the position of domestic airlines in the broad economic setting seemed to be that they were particularly unaffected by the vicissitudes of the national economy. Although there exists some relationship between disposable personal income and expenditure on air travel, the relative independence of airline revenues from such changes has been explained as owing to an overriding growth trend in the industry.

Much emphasis is put on this apparently favored position of the airline industry. One reads of "industry" recessions, independent of the state of the national economy, and of airline revenue and activity remaining high during periods of national recession. In 1958, when

[13] Cf. *ibid.*, pp. 89 ff.

TABLE 2-6. DOMESTIC TRUNKLINE REVENUES

(All in thousands)

Year	Passenger	Per Cent of Total	U.S. Mail	Per Cent of Total	Express and Freight	Per Cent of Total	Other[a]	Per Cent of Total	Total
1946	272,573	87.39	20,274	6.50	13,270	4.26	5,776	1.85	311,893
1947	303,194	86.01	23,326	6.62	18,888	5.36	7,083	2.01	352,490
1948	334,736	80.98	47,838	11.57	23,789	5.76	6,991	1.69	413,353
1949	378,113	82.24	45,031	9.79	27,281	5.93	9,358	2.04	459,783
1950	430,098	82.06	46,311	8.84	34,267	6.54	13,432	2.56	524,109
1951	570,288	86.60	37,040	5.62	35,736	5.43	15,457	2.35	658,521
1952	671,257	87.40	35,910	4.68	41,382	5.39	19,465	2.54	768,015
1953	775,782	88.28	37,083	4.22	46,170	5.25	19,758	2.25	878,793
1954	872,834	89.23	37,310	3.81	48,114	4.92	19,956	2.04	978,214
1955	1,021,855	90.16	30,130	2.66	59,010	5.21	22,353	1.97	1,133,348
1956	1,142,197	90.45	34,200	2.71	60,274	4.77	26,160	2.07	1,262,831
1957	1,287,172	90.67	34,944	2.46	64,537	4.55	32,961	2.32	1,419,614
1958	1,362,992	90.07	38,501	2.55	73,491	4.85	38,265	2.53	1,513,249
1959	1,632,646	90.77	40,576	2.26	86,183	4.79	39,204	2.18	1,798,609
1960	1,756,439	90.42	44,768	2.30	96,577	4.97	44,850	2.31	1,942,634

a. Includes revenues from excess baggage and from charter operations, and incidental revenues.

Source: Revenue figures from various issues of Air Transport Association, *Air Transport Facts and Figures, passim.*

the annual GNP receded sharply, airline traffic dipped below 1957 levels in only a few months and ended the year with only a 3 per cent drop. Moreover, much of the 1958 decline, especially in the fourth quarter, has been attributed to the airline industry strikes.[14] This led airline observers to contrast the position of the airlines with other forms of transport:

> Airline traffic normally does not react sharply to short-term disruptions in the economy. Industry traffic held firm during the steel strike while the railroads are attributing 1959's decline in earnings to that strike.[15]

In the 1954 business decline, when the annual gross national product dipped below levels reached in the previous year, airline traffic continued to expand, although the rate of expansion was somewhat slower than it had been in previous years.

In 1949 there is a coincidence of recessions in GNP and in the airline industry, although the latter is usually explained as being independent of the former. The airline situation in 1949, it may be argued, was the logical result of a series of actions over the preceding three years. The end of World War II found the domestic airlines optimistic and enthusiastic about their operations in the next few years. Demand had far outrun available capacity during the war years, and the airlines saw no reason for it to decline with the return to peacetime conditions. Consequently, there was a scramble for new route applications and new aircraft equipment orders. Military DC-3's and DC-4's were rapidly converted to commercial operation. These were either purchased or leased by the airlines, and usually they required a substantial additional investment in modifications in order to meet airline safety and equipment standards. Shortly thereafter, new equipment began to be delivered.

The period of optimism lasted scarcely more than a year; yet traffic had indeed increased. The disturbing item was that available capacity had been increased even more. In the face of increasing traffic, the over-all load factors read 88.12 per cent in 1945, 78.81 per cent in

[14] *Aviation Week*, February 29, 1960, p. 38. The following strikes occurred in the domestic trunkline industry in 1958: American, 12/20/58–1/11/59; Capital, 10/17/58–11/23/58; Eastern, 11/24/58–1/2/59; Trans World, 11/21/58–12/8/58; Western, 2/22/58–6/10/58. From U.S. Civil Aeronautics Board, *Monthly Report of Air Carrier Traffic Statistics*, November, 1959, p. 51.

[15] *Aviation Week*, February 29, 1960, p. 38.

1946, and 65.67 per cent in 1947.[16] Whereas costs per *available* ton-mile[17] decreased (32.29 cents in 1946; 31.21 cents in 1947), the costs per *revenue* ton-mile[18] moved in the opposite direction (48.78 cents in 1946; 54.64 cents in 1947).

Moreover, 1947 was plagued with a number of major accidents; public confidence was badly shaken.[19] In November, 1947, the new DC-6 was grounded pending safety compliance examinations; Lockheed Constellations and Martin aircraft also had serious problems. Costs continued to rise with the general price level following removal of wartime controls.[20] Thus rising costs, high accident rates, and

[16] Cherington, *op. cit.*, p. 85.

[17] Costs divided by a figure that measures transport capacity available.

[18] Costs divided by a figure that represents transport capacity actually used.

[19] The following table shows that 1947 was bad by almost any standards.

Year	Fatal Accidents	Passenger Fatalities	Passenger-Miles Flown per Passenger Fatality (000)	Passenger Fatalities per 100 Million Passenger-Miles
1946	9	75	80,895	1.2
1947	5	199	31,697	3.2
1948	5	83	75,035	1.3
1949	4	93	76,033	1.3
1950	4	96	87,119	1.1

Source: Adapted from Frederick, *op. cit.*, Table 33, p. 333.

[20] The following table shows equipment cost trends through 1949:

Equipment	Year and Quarter		Cost
Lockheed 049	1946	1	$684,398
		2	705,624
		4	785,940
Lockheed 649	1947	3	754,930
Lockheed 749	1948	2	870,690
		4	923,033
	1949	4	1,076,940
Douglas DC-4	1946	2	366,500
	1947	1	447,828
DC-6	1946	4	587,554
	1947	3	627,210
		4	655,772
	1948	3	678,322
	1949	4	751,396
Convair 240	1947	1	134,640
		3	200,038
		4	282,990
	1949	1	299,658
Martin 202	1947	3	247,356
		4	333,242

All prices include one set of engines only and no spare parts. Data from U.S., Congress, House, Subcommittee of the Committee on Interstate and Foreign Commerce, *Hearings, on HR-4648, 4677, 8902, and 8903, Civil Air Policy*, 84th Cong., 1st and 2nd Sess., 1955–1956, pp. 585–586.

rapid expansion of equipment all may have contributed to the low 1947–1949 revenue picture for the airlines.

All this served as a satisfactory explanation of events throughout the late 1940's and the decade of the 1950's. Nothing really seemed to contradict it. During the first half of 1960, however, the economy did not exhibit the bounce that many had forecast. In fact, a slight dip occurred. Simultaneously, airline traffic fell below that which had been predicted, and it caused some consternation among airline industry observers:

> The trend during the first six months of the year [1960] is an enigmatic departure from traditional growth patterns set by the airlines industry in the past. *Normally*, trunkline traffic tends to remain fairly stable in times of general business recession. . . . It is the general feeling among a large number of airline economists that airline business should follow a growth pattern even in periods when the general economy settles on temporary plateaus. As a result . . ., industry executives are finding it difficult to pin down some reason for the disappointing showing during the first half of 1960.[21]

In fact, by early 1961, one reads that "airline business is extremely sensitive to the fluctuations of the Gross National Product. . . ."[22]

It will be suggested here that what has been regarded as normal in the past may have been highly abnormal. It could well be that the airlines were on the crest of a wave of technological good fortune for more than a decade and that by 1961 they began settling down to a position similar to that which most industries have occupied for years, namely, one dependent upon the general economic climate.

Demand Elasticity

Economists have realized for some time that observations of prices ruling and quantities purchased of a particular product at various points in time do not necessarily tell them much about the nature of the demand curve for that product.[23] Shifts of the curve, in response to any number of nonprice stimuli, have frequently plagued researchers

[21] *Aviation Week*, July 18, 1960, p. 40, italics mine.

[22] *Aviation Week*, January 30, 1961, p. 36.

[23] This was pointed out early by E. J. Working, "What Do Statistical 'Demand Curves' Show?," *Quarterly Journal of Economics*, XLI (February, 1927), 212–235, also reprinted in George J. Stigler and Kenneth E. Boulding (eds.), *Readings in Price Theory* ("Republished Articles on Economics," Vol. VII; Homewood: Richard D. Irwin, Inc., 1952), pp. 97–115.

interested in the probable effects of various price policies. Furthermore, demand for air travel is actually divisible into at least two major classes, personal and business, both of which are further divisible. This makes any discussion of *the* elasticity of demand for air travel already an aggregative and necessarily more imprecise concept.[24]

This study cannot go deeply into the question of elasticity in the air travel market. That is a separate topic in itself. A brief survey will be presented of those comments which have come to this writer's attention.

a. Nicholson occasionally uses the term elasticity in an imprecise way, but his general conclusions would seem to be that demand for air travel is elastic (at least downward).[25]

b. Frederick's comments are also of a general nature, again suggesting some elasticity of demand or at least not inelasticity. After stating that volume of business will increase with decreases in airline rates (which of course can happen whether elasticity of demand is greater than, equal to, or less than unity), he continues:

> No data is available on the exact elasticity of demand . . . for airline service; but there is reason to believe that the elasticity is relatively high, because of the existence of substitute forms of transportation.[26]

There may be reason to believe that elasticity is relatively high, but the existence of substitutes is probably not the strongest evidence for it. It is relevant only when considering an increase in price, and it may not even be relevant then. The airlines will argue, for example, especially for medium and long hauls, that the advantages of air travel are such as to make alternative modes of transport very poor substitutes for their product. This is especially true now. Jet aircraft have produced significant time advantages in all but the very short-haul markets.

c. Cherington has gathered rather general and extensive evidence on reactions in particular markets to price adjustments in the postwar period. He concludes that, for a particular class of service, demand is

[24] Edward J. Taaffe emphasized the possible importance of the concept of elasticity over a given route and differentials in elasticity for different types of routes in "Trends in Airline Passenger Traffic: A Geographic Case Study," *Annals of the Association of American Geographers*, XLIX (December, 1959), 393–408, and in correspondence with this writer, June 1, 1960.

[25] Nicholson, *op. cit.*, pp. 201, 203.

[26] Frederick, *op. cit.*, p. 167.

rather inelastic for price changes in either direction. However, he continues:

> Although the demand for air travel appears to be relatively inelastic so far as small price changes within a particular market are concerned, the substantial growth of coach traffic in recent years indicates that under differential pricing (multiple classes of service or levels of fares), the total demand of all markets may be elastic in that markets can be added and total revenues increased with comparatively little diversion or trading down of higher yield traffic.[27]

It seems more meaningful to consider the demands in the separate coach and first-class markets as distinct functions. This avoids the dangers inherent in aggregating to produce a single demand curve for domestic air travel. Furthermore, with the increasing delivery of jet equipment and consequent removal of more and more piston equipment from service, essentially only two types of service (and pricing) are emerging on domestic flights. Usually these are on the same aircraft, and they are distinguished almost exclusively by service extras such as meals and seating space. Thus Cherington's conclusions of inelasticity in each market are of more interest than those concerning *total* demand.

d. There is some discussion of elasticity in the evidence presented by various airlines in the lengthy *General Passenger Fare Investigation.* Here there is at least one detailed discussion, ostensibly of the theoretical concept of elasticity as well as its application to the air transport industry. Reference is made to testimony made for American Airlines by Robert E. Kimble.[28]

The general question to which the analysis is addressed is the following: What could be the effect on airline revenues of an increase in fares of approximately 15 per cent? The conclusion is that such an increase would not harm revenues. Mr. Kimble must feel that, at the point at which fares were set in 1957, the airlines were operating in an inelastic part of the general demand curve for their product. Indeed, he feels that airline demand is inelastic, but the reasoning involved does not lend confidence to the result. To the present writer, elasticity of demand has always been a static concept; i.e., it deals with probable

[27] Cherington, *op. cit.*, p. 439.

[28] American Airlines, Exhibit AA-12, "Testimony of Robert E. Kimble," in *General Passenger Fare Investigation.*

reactions on a given, unchanging curve. However, in Kimble's analysis the decisive factor seems to be lodged in dynamic changes.

> About all that can be said about the elasticity of airline demand . . . is that the elasticity of demand has been steadily declining if the slopes of the individual demand curves are the same. If airline demand has been shifting so that the slope of the curve is unchanged throughout the period, then it is virtually certain that the demand for air transportation at the 1956 average yield is inelastic. . . . It is more likely, of course that the slope has not remained the same throughout the passage of time. Nonetheless, unless the slope has changed substantially during the period, the demand at current price levels would still be inelastic.[29]
>
> All these observations support the belief that the demand for air transportation has been shifting at a very substantial rate and consequently that demand is relatively inelastic. Substantial shifts in demand, unless they can be specifically correlated with relative changes in the prices of competitive products, almost necessarily indicate inelasticity of demand.[30]

The relationship between shifts in demand and elasticity is assuredly not as thoroughly accepted as Kimble implies. A particular point on a particular demand curve has an elasticity that can be measured or estimated. Steep or flat straight lines may be generally characterized as inelastic or elastic, respectively, although even this is not strictly correct, and a rectangular hyperbola has unitary elasticity at every point. The position that Kimble is taking involves strict and unrealistic assumptions about the constant nature of the demand curves over time. For a straight-line curve that intersects the x-axis at point Q and the y-axis at point D, the elasticity at a point P on the curve is defined as PQ/PD.[31] Then if a horizontal line is drawn at some constant ruling price, and if the demand curve shifts rightward in a number of steps, always parallel to the original curve, the elasticity at each of these succeeding points will be smaller than at any of the previous ones.[32] There is some geometrical logic to this position, but there are too many factors involved in the shifting of demand curves over time (including the problem of correctly identifying such shifts)

[29] *Ibid.*, pp. 7–8.

[30] *Ibid.*, pp. 10–11.

[31] Note that Kimble formulates this correctly and then makes the erroneous statement that if the elasticity at a point is 0.5, the point would be located one-half of the distance from Q to D. See *ibid.*, p. 4.

[32] The numerator of PQ/PD remains constant, the denominator is increasing.

to imply any general connection between demand curve shifts and elasticity.

e. In the same investigation, United Air Lines denies the possibility of anything like measurability of elasticity and instead makes purely intuitive statements:

> The third matter for consideration is the effect of the increase in fares of 17% upon our market. There is no precise way of determining in advance what such an effect will be. Lacking any scientific approach to this question it then becomes largely a matter of judgement. In our judgement the increase in fares which we propose will have no appreciable effect upon our market.[33]

The brief discussion following this hinges on the fact that the "intelligent and discerning" public which demands air travel will continue to recognize it as a bargain.[34]

Thus, two of the largest airlines conclude that the demand for air travel is inelastic and that price increases will not harm and probably will help revenues.[35] One uses inaccurate reasoning, the other simply makes a statement. Of more importance, regardless of the methods which they employ, is the fact that two of the Big Four trunklines (and most probably also many other trunks) act *as if* the demand for their product were inelastic; e.g., they advocate price increases.

3. Market Structure and Market Performance

It is well to pause at this point and indicate the general goals toward which this analysis is working. In simplified terms, the study hopes to arrive at an efficient (least-cost) scheduling of available types of aircraft over selected domestic routes, given actual demands for specified

[33] United Air Lines, Exhibit U-9, "Testimony of Robert E. Johnson," p. 20, in *General Passenger Fare Investigation.*

[34] *Ibid.*, pp. 20, 22.

[35] The elasticity discussions are also commented upon in "Initial Decision of Examiner Ralph L. Wiser" in *General Passenger Fare Investigation.* Although the statements about elasticity do not always specifically say so, they concern themselves almost exclusively with an *increase* in fares. In commenting on the apparently low observed elasticity of demand (lack of response to fare decreases) in the European air travel market, Wheatcroft (*op. cit.*, pp. 169–170) suggests that there exists an appreciable time lag between reductions and public reaction, so that the reductions of 1953 should be judged at least in part by their influence on traffic developments in 1954 and 1955. But this seems to stretch the elasticity concept beyond its proper limits. It is concerned with more immediate changes in quantity demanded in response to price changes. The changes one or two years later surely are more likely explained by shift of the demand curve. Elasticity should concern itself with shifts on a given demand curve.

years. Comparisons should then be possible between actual allocation and the very ideal allocations developed here. It seems not unsafe to assume that there will be a discrepancy; it will be of interest to inquire into the particular causes from which this difference arises and, if possible, to weigh these various causes according to their importance.

The following more general question is also relevant. Assume that the cost of the actual allocation over routes considered was X dollars more expensive than the ideal (or some modification of the ideal cost in the direction of realism). Then, was the amount X a reasonable price to pay for the assurance of regulation in an industry where without such regulation the allocation would have been worse and thus more costly? In other words: Is it clear that the allocation would have been worse? What would the industry provide if left to its own devices; would the unregulated market solution differ from the ideal allocation by a greater or smaller amount than the actual regulated one?

The domestic airline industry today is supervised in two broad areas. These cover economic regulation and safety regulation. Clearly, there is a broad latitude for the application of general regulatory principles in both of these areas. However, within a wide range, the results will be influenced in varying proportions both by the fact of regulation and also by the underlying economic structure of the industry to which it is applied.[36] The end points, or bounds, of this range of possibilities will be: (1) complete freedom from regulation on the one hand, and (2) complete government regulation on the other, i.e., competition or government monopoly. As a matter of practical reality, the latter may be dismissed almost immediately as being not compatible with current public opinion. Furthermore, there seems to be nothing in the character of airline operations which automatically creates a natural monopoly situation, as was discussed in Section 1.

In those cases where monopoly is not the natural outcome of the technical environment, can government establishment of complete control be justified? Fellner makes a general statement that is relevant to the situation here considered:

> The gradual narrowing of oligopoly into monopoly is justifiable in those exceptional cases where the technical economies of monopolistic

[36] "It might be said that regulatory policy sets the limits of potential competition within which managerial decision sets the extent of actual competition," E. J. Taaffe, "A Map Analysis of United States Airline Competition: I — The Development of Competition," *Journal of Air Law and Commerce*, XXV (Spring, 1958), 147.

concentration are substantial up to the extreme degree of concentration and where the avoidance of uncertainty is so important that even "oligopolistic uncertainty" is excessive. . . . The deliberate establishment of government-supervised monopolies in certain areas (utilities, communication, and so forth) should presumably be attributed to the conviction that, in the areas in question, these conditions are satisfied. Where these conditions are not satisfied, monopoly is inferior to oligopoly, from the social point of view, and narrow oligopoly (which approximates monopoly more closely) is inferior to broader oligopoly (in which the competitive element is likely to be stronger).[37]

It is here argued that regularity of service will come about of its own accord, and that government-established monopoly is an unnatural and unnecessary means to this end. One need only look at the results of the competitive pressures as they now exist in the industry, especially over a particular high-density route, and at the service which has come about during approximately the last fifteen years. One can argue that potential competition is in many cases strong enough to assure reasonable regularity, even on the less important routes.[38] Keyes concludes, writing in 1955:

As a result of a study undertaken some years ago [1950], the present writer concluded that no available evidence or argument showed a need for the existing type of Federal control over entry into air transport markets, although it was conceivable that future experience might show that some limit on competitive freedom would be necessary to safeguard a desirable degree of regularity in air transport service. Since that time, experience has served to confirm the conclusion and remove the qualification . . . competitive pressures in the air transport field are a powerful force working toward rather than away from greater regularity of service. . . .

It is not surprising, therefore, that the argument for protective certification based on regularity of service is no longer fashionable.[39]

Furthermore, there is a strong *a priori* case that can be made against the general adoption of any policy involving complete elimination of

[37] William Fellner, *Competition Among the Few* (New York: Alfred A. Knopf, 1949), pp. 290–291.

[38] Less so on the local service routes. These, by their very nature, are the shorter routes for which potential competition from other forms of transportation is much more effective.

[39] L. S. Keyes, "A Reconsideration of Federal Control of Entry into Air Transportation," *Journal of Air Law and Commerce*, XXII (Spring, 1955), 196.

competition. Although the dangers of unfettered competition may be acknowledged, there are also dangers of monopoly. It will be suggested here that these dangers, e.g., tendencies to stagnation and deadening of initiative, are even greater than those connected with free competition. Clearly, there is currently a good deal of service and "quality" competition between domestic trunklines, perhaps too much. Some observers, however, make a rational defense of much that this competition has produced:

> It is not . . . true that all competition in this field is wasteful, for it is the essential claim for competition that it will produce the best possible quality that the consumer wishes to pay for. . . . The quality of airline service will be determined by the type of aeroplane used, its speed, pressurization, comfort; the convenience of schedules, their frequency, timing, connections, number of stops; the passenger cabin service, the meals, steward service, size and arrangement of seats and the passenger ground services such as the reservations service, ground transport, baggage handling, and so on.[40]

Of course, "best" possible quality may receive many different interpretations, and it is clear that any particular quality improvement can be carried to excesses, but it is much less clear where this point of excess might begin. It is suggested that the general case that can be made against monopoly is a stronger one than can be made against competition, and the discussion therefore turns to a consideration of complete nonregulation.

It is clear from Section 1 that the operation of economies of scale in the airline industry is more related to density of the traffic than to particular absolute size of the carrier. A high traffic volume over a given route permits high load factors and encourages high daily utilization of equipment.[41] The numerous ways of inducing product differences — service, speed, equipment — and the high costs of entry plus the size of many existing firms all suggest the probable

[40] Wheatcroft, *op. cit.*, p. 226.

[41] Here again the position of the Big Four is decisive. The per cent of each group's total traffic that is made up of passengers enplaned at stations with 5,000 or more passengers per month (i.e., high traffic-generating nodes) was as follows in 1955: Big Four — 87.5 per cent; Middle Six — 69.4 per cent; Little Three — 46.4 per cent. (The composition of these groups has changed somewhat since 1955 with the merger of Colonial and Eastern, Capital and United.) U.S., Congress, House, *Report of the Antitrust Subcommittee on the Judiciary pursuant to H.R. 107 (Airlines)*, 85th Cong., 1st Sess., p. 111.

emergence of no more domestic trunklines than now exist, and perhaps fewer, should all regulation be removed.[42]

It is of interest to note that this conclusion has become more certain as the technology of air transport has progressed. The sizable investments required of a potential entrant into the industry are largely responsible for this. It has recently been estimated that, for a prospective trunk airline to achieve a fully competitive position in a single major domestic traffic market, a minimum investment of $15 million in aircraft and ground facilities would be required.[43] This is not the sort of operation that becomes workable overnight. And in this sense the character of the industry has changed appreciably in the last fifteen years, since the end of World War II when relatively inexpensive used military aircraft plus wartime flying and/or mechanical experience were major steps toward complete operationality.

The modern expensive jet aircraft is responsible for another trend that also is operating in favor of a smaller rather than a larger number of firms in the domestic trunkline industry. It is simply that the absolute number of passengers necessary to break even with a given type of aircraft has increased with the introduction of jet aircraft. To be sure, the announced claims of a reduction in break-even load factors may be technologically quite valid. However, a decreased percentage of an increased number of available seats may result in either a smaller or a larger number of passengers. In fact, the latter is true. For the years 1953–1956, the actual load factor on all domestic trunkline operations was around 64 per cent; the required break-even load factor is reported to have been around 56 per cent.[44] Of the *largest* four engine aircraft operating during this period, the Douglas DC-7 and the Lockheed L-1049 "Constellation" are representative. Seating

[42] Note that interest here centers on domestic trunks that, by definition, are long-range, nonlocal carriers. Bigness is inherent in the name itself.

[43] United Research Incorporated, *Federal Regulation of the Domestic Air Transport Industry* (Cambridge: United Research Incorporated, 1959), p. 118. This was for the New York-Miami run at 1958 traffic levels. It posited two 707 aircraft, utilized 13 hours per day, at initial cost of $6.5 million each, including spares, plus minimum ground facilities of $750,000 at each end of the run. Earlier discussion was concerned with the position of airlines relative to other forms of transport. The absolute level, even for the airlines, is high.

[44] Stanley Gewirtz, "Dynamic Air Transport: A Study in Growth in Service and Growth in Competition." (Condensation of testimony before the Antitrust Subcommittee of the House Judiciary Committee), (mimeographed, n.d.,) p. 21B; Boeing Airplane Company, "Jet Airliners: Economics and World Markets" (multilithed, n.d.), *passim.*

configurations vary greatly on these two aircraft, the stated range on the first being 54 to 89, the second 64 to 88.[45]

If the case is biased as far as possible toward the currently popular jets by taking the upper end of the piston-plane passenger range,[46] the result is simply (0.56)(89) = 49.8, or an average of 50 passengers (at the very most) necessary to break even in 1953–1956. One aircraft manufacturer presents charts intended to show the trend and magnitude of operating costs for typical piston and jet equipment with different ranges of operation. The presentation is in terms of passengers necessary to break even on a given type of aircraft. While it shows a rapid drop as the range of the aircraft is increased, the number of passengers necessary to break even is always at least 5 greater for a medium-range jet, as compared with a medium-range piston plane, and 10 larger for a long-range jet, as compared with piston equipment of similar range. At the time of writing, there is no domestic trunkline operating experience with medium-range jets,[47] but the break-even load factor on a long-range jet (Boeing 707-120) has been reported as 41 per cent.[48] For the manufacturer's specification of 136 seats,[49] then (0.41)(136) = 55.76, or 56 passengers are needed. This is at the very least a 12 per cent increase in passengers necessary to break even.

At best, the introduction of jet service may have resulted in some increase in the total number of people traveling by air; i.e., new markets may have been tapped.[50] Whether domestic air travel will

[45] *American Aviation*, April 22, 1957, pp. 123–124.

[46] That is, applying the stated piston break-even load factor to the nonjet configuration carrying the largest number of people. This obviously gives the highest number of passengers necessary in the prejet era. Moreover, (1) the largest aircraft for the period have been chosen; no average type has been selected to reflect the smaller twin-engine craft that were in frequent use; (2) the aircraft most representative of (large) equipment in the *last* year of the period (1956) have been used.

[47] It is interesting that the Boeing study just cited in footnote 44, makes a statement regarding the medium-range (and not yet operating) jets but not about the long-range ones. Namely: "A medium range piston airplane will break even with 28 passengers (47 per cent load factor). A medium range jet airplane will break even with 33 passengers (31 per cent load factor)," Boeing Airplane Company, *op. cit.*, p. 19.

[48] Experience of Continental Air Lines. Stated in *Aviation Week*, December 14, 1959, p. 25.

[49] Boeing Airplane Company, *op. cit.*, *passim*. This was composed of 47 first-class and 89 tourist-class passengers. Some airlines have been known to increase over-all carrying capacity by putting in more tourist space at the cost of reduced first-class space. For each two first-class seats removed, at least three tourist-class (and frequently more, due to decreased distance between the seats) passengers can be accommodated. Thus 136 may not be the top range, whereas 89 in the previous example definitely was.

[50] Even this guarded statement will be unacceptable to some industry observers. Cf., for example, *Aviation Week*, March 13, 1961, p. 146: "[turbojets have] . . . merely

continue to grow sufficiently in the future to keep these aircraft operating economically as they flood the market does not seem perfectly clear. Thus there may well exist this second characteristic of new equipment (in addition to its high initial cost) which suggests the presence of economic pressures working toward reduction of the total number of trunklines providing economically sound service.[51]

What might be expected, then, of this inherently oligopolistic industry, if it were left free of outside regulation or interference of any sort? It has been estimated that only a limited part of the entire domestic air travel market can economically sustain competitive services, i.e., is able to generate enough traffic to justify more than one carrier.[52] The most recent figures are the following: 350 to 400 of the 530 cities receiving air service (1958) can support the service of one carrier only, in terms of total demand generated and capabilities of modern equipment. Furthermore, subsidization is necessary to make the services at approximately 300 of these points economically feasible. At most, about 100 cities generate sufficient traffic to support the services of two or more carriers.[53] These figures suggest a possible division of domestic air travel points:

1. Cities which are generally small and which do not generate sufficient passenger demand to support profitably the services of even a single carrier on any regular basis — local service carrier points.

2. Medium-sized cities which may be termed natural monopoly areas in that they produce sufficient traffic to support only a single carrier economically.

---

resulted in a diversion from piston-engine aircraft rather than opening of new markets or in an expanding traffic volume, which more than one top airline official said would be the case."

[51] A basically similar conclusion is stated in United Research Incorporated, *op. cit.*, p. 117.

[52] This and the discussion that follows draw on facts presented in *ibid.* This does not imply agreement with policy recommendations contained in that source. Among other sources dealing with airline competition, the following pay particular attention to the question of whether much of the CAB authorized competitive services were or are justified on grounds of existing demand: Frederick W. Gill and Gilbert L. Bates, *Airline Competition* (Cambridge: Harvard University Printing Office, 1949); Herbert H. Whitehead, "Effects of Competition and Changes in Route Structure on Growth of Domestic Air Travel," *Journal of Air Law and Commerce*, XVIII (Winter, 1951), 78–90; and David W. Bluestone, "The Problem of Competition Among Domestic Trunk Airlines," *Journal of Air Law and Commerce*, XX and XXI (Autumn, 1953), 379–402, and (Winter, 1954), 50–87.

[53] United Research Incorporated, *op. cit.*, p. i. These points are ones that are served by trunklines, not local service carriers.

3. Largest markets where traffic generation is great enough to sustain the services of two or more carriers — trunkline points.

Within such a framework, it is not difficult to indicate the probable behavior that might be expected in each of these market types, should regulation be removed. The smallest cities would assuredly experience reductions in service; it would become less regular and frequent, if indeed it did not disappear completely in many cases of very weak traffic generation.[54] There is no reason to assume, however, that all service to all of these points would be discontinued, for at least two reasons: First, an individual airline might be able to increase fares sufficiently to make the route indeed a profitable one. This presupposes an inelasticity of demand appropriate to bring about the desired result — an assumption that is not unrealistic, as Section 2 has shown. Second, service might be continued without a profit or even at a loss because of the particular growth potential that the airline could believe to exist at the city or on the route segment in question. In such cases there might be a large amount of experimentation with and testing of the market potential in different areas. This would imply a period of intermittency and irregularity of service but with a final result of perhaps only slightly curtailed service at no significant increase in price.

For those cities in classification 2, there is perhaps a presumption toward deterioration of service, or increase of price, or both. It is not unlikely that sufficient *potential* competition would exist to avoid excessive abuses of this sort. However, fare instability might occur insofar as the individual monopolist on a particular route could experiment with how much of a price increase could be sustained before the attendant profits drew competitive action and retaliation. Similarly, potential competition might not only check service or equipment deterioration but even improve it. However, this would be secondary, no doubt, to the better equipment and service impetus that would obtain on the routes of class 3, those that are indeed competitive. Here behavior would be very similar to that which now occurs, under government regulation, on the long-haul, high-density

[54] Professor Jesse Markham correctly points out that the marginal cost of serving a small city may be much lower than the average cost of serving *only* small cities. It will be argued here, however, that the independence which is assumed between markets (especially between 1 and 3) is not unrealistic. Trunklines and local service airlines fulfill basically different functions.

routes. Equipment and service rivalry are already strong. The major difference here would probably be in the field of fare experimentation, both with the levels of fares and also with their structure. That is, it is possible that effort would be made to subdivide the market into different and distinct components with appropriately differing fares. The tendency would probably be toward fare cutting in an effort to capture a larger segment of the total market in question.[55]

Another general possibility that deserves mention is pooling of equipment and facilities. There is a small amount of leasing currently, but clearly greater use could be made of the pooling concept, whereby equipment was transferred from one carrier to another as demand fluctuated over specific routes. This has the advantage of producing more effective utilization of capacity where it is needed, thereby reducing excess capacity.[56] Further, operating costs are reduced through such utilization as well as through the elimination of duplications of traffic and operational staffs at particular stations and the possible reduction of effort and expenditures on sales promotion and advertising.[57]

An important trend is emerging, however. Although just beginning, it will undoubtedly gain strength in the next few years. This is the merger of trunklines, and it carries with it many implications for the industry. Note that such mergers are in effect pooling arrangements whereby equipment is more generally available over a wider system and personnel are reduced. For example, the United-Capital merger (1961) extends a major East–West carrier into the seasonal Southeast and allows an over-all easy interchange of equipment as demand warrants it. In fact, mergers are a solution to many financial problems

[55] It might be argued that each airline would aim at an equal rate of profit on each of its individual routes. This would be a general rate structure problem that would be attacked through differential changes in fares, depending on the strength (and "character," elasticity of demand, potential, etc.) of each particular route. See United Research Incorporated, *op. cit.*, p. 71: "If the Board has never paid extensive attention to the level of passenger fares, it has given still less attention to the structure of fares, except as the structure is affected by the Board's surveillance over questions of discrimination, preference or prejudice."

[56] Wheatcroft, *op. cit.*, pp. 259 ff., states that such claims are not supported by available European evidence, but the evidence in question is sketchy. Three airlines in Mexico claim that six aircraft can do the work of eight in an equipment pool arrangement. See *Aviation Week*, November 28, 1960, pp. 43–45.

[57] The strength of these savings depends of course on how complete such pooling arrangements are. Wheatcroft, *op. cit.*, suggests that most of them may be achieved by other means as well and mentions subcontracting. To the present writer this seems rather unlikely.

that plague domestic trunklines, especially now with high-capacity, high-speed jet equipment generating a great deal of new seat-mile capacity. They have long been advocated by some airline executives as beneficial to the individual operators themselves. From a more over-all point of view they also are advantageous in at least providing the setting for a more efficient use of equipment and thereby also an efficient route structure. If merger action is generally sanctioned by the CAB, and if a number of airlines do merge, then a great deal of the problem of efficiency of route structure will be solved.[58] It is not yet clear how generally popular such action will be among the airlines.

Some writers have argued that unregulated competition may lead to undesirable and dangerous operating practices within certain airlines. There could be a tendency to become lax in certain operating and safety measures. This would be especially tempting to the carriers that were financially less strong when obvious cost savings or increased equipment utilization would result. Indeed this was another of the major reasons for the original Civil Aeronautics Act. Clearly, no airline will be willing to risk its reputation and jeopardize its position by cutting corners excessively, but moves in this direction might be tempting. There is no reason, however, why adequate safety regulation cannot be devised to handle this question without bringing it into the sphere of economic regulation and policy. That is, deterioration of safety standards need not be related to whether or not competition in the industry is regulated.[59]

As far as excess capacity is concerned, the threat of competition on the more active routes, insofar as it leads to less freedom for fare increases and to a tendency toward keeping prices relatively low, might lead also to an interest in lowering costs in order to maintain some sort of profit. This could be a factor conducive to some more careful equipment scheduling and consequently to a reduction in excess capacity.

If the airlines had never experienced any regulation, then the

[58] The trend seems to be in the direction of Board approval of mergers. In 1961 it not only approved the United-Capital union but seems to be seeking a partner for Northeast as well. See *Aviation Week*, June 19, 1961, p. 39. For general discussion on the merits of merger in the domestic air transport industry and against excessive government regulation and interference, see relevant sections of Federal Aviation Agency, *Report of the Task Force on National Aviation Goals* ("Project Horizon") (Washington, D. C.: U.S. Government Printing Office, 1961).

[59] Keyes, *op. cit.*, pp. 196–197, argues this same position strongly.

preceding might be satisfactory suggestions regarding unregulated market behavior in that industry. The fear of precisely such service instabilities and rate cutting were prominent among the reasons presented in arguing for the Civil Aeronautics Act prior to its passage in 1938. To speak of "deregulation" now might imply any number of variants of a rather different type of behavior, especially on the most important routes, and in a sense perhaps also for the entire domestic system. A likely possibility would be some kind of more rigid collusion. It is conceivable that some attempts at retaining the existing shares of the market might be forthcoming on those routes where currently several lines provide service. Such behavior, should it be successful, might well be extended to entire regions and eventually to the entire domestic market. But the essential problem that provides the basic instability in such situations is of course the temptation to cheat a bit on the system. Mutual interdependence, although recognized, need not necessarily be thoroughly understood by each individual firm in the industry. Moreover, the current excesses of advertising aimed at the traveling public have succeeded in differentiating the product offered.[60] Thus it would be tempting, even in a situation of agreement among airlines, to attempt to profit by these real or imagined differences.

The following conclusion will be suggested. Although the history of the industry might imply a great deal of collusion, it is more likely that class 1 and 2 nodes would experience variation, irregularity, and some deterioration of service, while class 3, where initially some collusion seems most probable, would see possibly increased rivalry among firms with consequent service and/or fare advantages to the consumers at those points.

Equally great, if not greater, effects clearly would be felt by the airlines themselves. It has recently been suggested that from four to six final competitors would emerge in the industry following removal of all governmental regulation.[61] This may be extreme; however, it is quite possible that several of the financially weaker or more badly managed trunk airlines would find themselves eliminated. There is a strong further possibility that the emergent lines would attempt to

[60] For the view that the preferences of the air-traveling public do not attach themselves to particular airlines as such, see Lucien Foldes, "Domestic Air Transport Policy. II," *Economica* XXVIII (August, 1961), 277.

[61] United Research Incorporated, *op. cit.*, pp. 108 ff. Merger could have the same final result.

extend themselves into the regional areas, thereby threatening at least some of the local service airlines as well.

The above discussion has touched on what appear to be the most probable facets of behavior of firms in the domestic trunkline industry. The results are shown to be far from purely competitive in any accepted sense of the phrase, and they exhibit certain unpleasant features (i.e., irregularities, higher fares) for the avoidance of which the public may well be willing to pay some amount. A relevant later question will center around how large this amount might be.

4. Summary

The study of any phase of domestic trunkline industry operations should proceed from a clear understanding of the economic character of that industry and of the regulatory environment within which it functions. The former has been examined in this chapter. The cost conditions in the industry indicate what is involved in minimizing total direct operating costs; they also provide a basis for comments on possible economies of scale and thus for speculations about the behavior of the domestic trunkline industry if all government economic regulation were to be removed. The nature of airline revenues and especially the discussions of elasticity of demand in this industry help to support conclusions reached in this chapter. There seems to be some technical justification to the position that complete competitive freedom is not an unreasonable alternative to current regulation and that some liberalization of government interference would be a logical first step. A more detailed examination of the regulatory setting provides the material for the following chapter.

Chapter 3

The Regulation of Air Transportation

THIS CHAPTER provides further background on which the rest of the study is projected. It suggests in some detail the lack of direction exhibited by regulatory policy in the air transportation industry. The mathematical methods developed in this study may help to fill this gap. Section 1 includes some general introductory comments. Section 2 presents the legal framework within which the various regulatory agencies concerned with this industry have worked.[1] In Section 3 some Civil Aeronautics Board decisions are cited, because they illustrate certain facets of regulatory policy that are especially relevant to this study. Appendix A presents comments on the philosophy of balanced competition under which the Board operates.

1. Introduction

In this chapter it will be suggested that the CAB has not always been consistent with regard to a number of points which come up repeatedly in route cases. It will further be implied that this is not only the result of varying interpretations given to over-all guiding standards or the methods of best achieving recognized aims, but that it also derives from the absence of clearly defined goals. The question

[1] An excellent comprehensive survey is available in United Research Incorporated, *Federal Regulation of the Domestic Air Transport Industry* (Cambridge: United Research Incorporated, 1959), Appendix A, "Legislative History of Major Economic Regulatory Provisions in Federal Civil Aviation Law."

of the efficiency of the domestic route structure and the emphasis that this concept has received will be of particular interest.

With respect to route award cases, it is necessary to make a basic distinction at the outset. The question of overscheduling on a given set of routes is the one in which this study is most interested. This is intimately related to the question of awarding additional carriers to routes that are already served by one or more airlines. There is, however, a second problem that frequently assumes major proportions in CAB route decisions. This is the question of the choice of carrier to receive a new award once the need for increased service has been established. Many of the major route cases begin when one carrier requests authorization to extend operations on the route in question. Seldom will all other trunklines let this request go unnoticed. Usually before the deadline for filing has arrived, all trunklines with operations in the general geographical area and those who feel that their interests are in some way at stake will have filed similar petitions. All carriers attempt to demonstrate the need for additional service, i.e., for an additional carrier. If the evidence is persuasive, the selection of a specific carrier then becomes a significant question.

Opinion bearing on both questions illustrates the lack of consistent reasoning which is often evident in Board decisions. The following quotations are representative of opinion which has been expressed in many places.[2]

[2] Additional comments that say much the same thing can be found in the following: Edward C. Sweeney, "Postwar International Route Planning by the Civil Aeronautics Board," *Journal of Air Law and Commerce*, XVI (Autumn, 1940), esp. 147; Russell B. Adams, "The Air Route Pattern Problem," *Journal of Air Law and Commerce*, XVII (Spring, 1950), esp. 127, 133; U.S., Congress, Senate, Committee on Interstate and Foreign Commerce, *Hearings, on S. 2647, Revision of Civil Aeronautics Act*, 83rd Cong., 2nd Sess., 1954, p. 528; Hardy K. Maclay and William C. Burt, "Entry of New Carriers into Domestic Trunkline Air Transportation," *Journal of Air Law and Commerce*, XXII (Spring, 1955), 138–139; M. George Goodrick, "The Air Route Problem in the United States," *Journal of Air Law and Commerce*, XVIII (Summer, 1951), 281, 294; LaMotte T. Cohu, "The Paradox of the Airlines," *Journal of Air Law and Commerce*, XV (Summer, 1948), 314–315; James A. Durham, "How Not to Regulate Air Transportation," *Law and Contemporary Problems*, XV (Winter, 1950), 114; "Civil Aeronautics Board Policy: An Evaluation," *Yale Law Journal*, LVII (April, 1948), 1083; U.S., Congress, Senate, Select Committee on Small Business, *Materials Relative to Competition in the Regulated Civil Aviation Industry*, 84th Cong., 2nd Sess., 1956, pp. 16–17; Stanley Berge, "Subsidies and Competition as Factors in Air Transport Policy," *American Economic Review*, XLI (May, 1951), 524; United Research Incorporated, *op. cit.*, p. viii; M. W. Heath, "Domestic Route Regulation by the CAB" (unpublished Ph.D. dissertation, University of Chicago, 1950), p. 296.

> In the case of new route certifications the Board's policy has evolved from case-to-case as exemplified by the Board's philosophy of competition. No general formulas or standards exist to show whether or not competition should or should not be instituted over a given route.
>
> . . . .
>
> The review of the Board's opinions granting additional service in new route and amendment cases illustrates its failure to develop and consistently apply adequate standards and its tendency to befog the economic policies.[3]
>
> . . . .
>
> An obvious fault in the Board's new route policy is a mechanical one arising out of the fact that it has not taken the initiative in planning the airline route pattern. Rather, it has simply decided cases as they have been presented as a result of the initiative of the carriers who file applications for new routes or extension.[4]

Roughly two periods of CAB action can be isolated as important from the point of view of route cases; these are from 1938 to about 1949 and from 1951 or 1952 to 1960.[5] The first period saw a general enthusiasm for experimentation and expansion of air carrier service which to a great extent strengthened the already large carriers. Although smaller inconsistencies are most certainly in evidence, the general goal of increased service by air carriers seems overwhelmingly present. For a few years there were no important route decisions made, but beginning in 1951 and clearly in evidence by 1953 there was a new interest in the strengthening of the relatively weak carriers.[6] Professor Caves has suggested that there exists a rather clear and definite *ordered* set of goals or objectives which the Board has before it, in effect, during all route cases. Strengthening the relatively weak

[3] Sweeney, *op. cit.*, pp. 132, 150, respectively.

[4] John H. Frederick, *Commercial Air Transportation* (4th ed.; Homewood: Richard D. Irwin, Inc., 1955), p. 198.

[5] This is the viewpoint presented in United Research Incorporated, *op. cit.* It was also suggested by Professor Richard Caves during discussions in May, 1960. A somewhat similar subdivision of periods with a different interpretation of Board action in the first period is found in Edward J. Taaffe, "A Map Analysis of United States Airline Competition: I. The Development of Competition," *Journal of Air Law and Commerce*, XV (Spring, 1958), 121–147. For example: "The most conspicuous thread of CAB policy running through both the first (1940–49) and the second (1954–56) waves of competitive increase has been that of strengthening the weak carrier . . . ," 146.

[6] The United Research study argues that even some of the measures enacted since 1951 to implement this inconsistent plan have been at cross purposes, e.g., extension of local service airlines among the least productive centers. See United Research Incorporated, *op. cit.*, pp. 31 ff.

carrier apparently tops the list. Furthermore, the question of individual or over-all route efficiency may be quite far down on that list.

Perhaps this is so. The following decisions may be contrasted and would seem to cast doubt on the consistency of Board action. In the *Southwest-Northeast Service Case* there are numerous clear statements indicating that the position of the weaker carriers deserves particular attention. The following is typical:

> . . . unless the relative economic opportunity — and basically this means route systems — of the smaller carrier approaches more closely that of the Big Four, their competitive position and ability to weather adversity are bound to suffer."[7]

The important fact is that the final decision made by the Board complemented these opinions.

Less than one year later the *New York-Florida Case* was settled.[8] On the surface, this decision was apparently designed to strengthen Northeast Airlines, which at that time was the only domestic trunkline still receiving government subsidy. Northeast received authorization into the New York-Miami route that included other important population centers as well. At the same time, "protection" was provided for Eastern Air Lines and National Airlines from the traffic diversion that Northeast might cause.[9] Not only does this run counter to the aim of strengthening Northeast, it also is difficult to reconcile with an earlier pronouncement on diversion. In the *New York-Chicago Service Case*, the CAB had disregarded the diverting effects of new competition from a carrier that was stronger than Northeast:

> Capital's proposed operation will not jeopardize the operations of the existing operators who possess competitive advantages in the form of historical participation in markets and greater resources.[10]

Regardless of relative positions on an ordered list, one might begin to question the consistency of Board logic. Admittedly, the Board was

[7] 22 CAB 52, 57 (1955).

[8] 24 CAB 94 (1956).

[9] These provisions were extensive. Eastern was given nonstop permission on flights between Boston and New York and Washington, making it a new and major competitor in Northeast's home market. All restrictions were also removed on Eastern's coastal runs to Florida, where formerly a number of prohibitions on nonstop and turnaround services had existed. Moreover, National's routes were extended from New York to Boston and Providence, and similar restrictions on the coastal route were removed.

[10] 22 CAB 973 (1955).

given much food for thought in Section 2 of the Civil Aeronautics Act. The terminology invites varying interpretation and, furthermore, includes numerous factors for consideration in each decision. The whole question of subsidy payments has influenced the attitude which the Board has taken on particular cases.[11] And its position on some degree of "balanced competition" in the industry has often seemed to dominate specific decisions.[12] Even if the Board has behaved in a broadly consistent manner with regard to the initial items in some sort of choice function, it is useful to indicate the manner in which the question of over-all route efficiency might be handled. Perhaps this consideration may someday move to a higher position on the list of objectives, when the others have been satisfactorily implemented.

2. The Regulatory Background

Before 1938

The Wright brothers made their historic flight at Kitty Hawk, North Carolina, on December 17, 1903. Early flying was looked upon largely as a sport, but by about 1911 one finds reference to the possibilities that airplanes offer for the transportation of mail in the annual reports of the Postmaster General.[13] After an initial period in which the Army carried the mail as a part of its general training program, it became apparent that efficiency might be improved if the Post Office handled the entire operation itself. It purchased its own airplanes and employed pilots to fly them. Routes were rapidly established between major East Coast cities and soon westward to Chicago

[11] The problem of government subsidy to air carriers in general and trunks in particular has been the basis for much discussion. It enters through the mail rate pay provisions of the Civil Aeronautics Act, and centers around the division of "service" mail pay and "need" mail pay — the former to be for actual mail carriage, the latter as subsidy over those routes on which the carrier involved is not making a profit. There are many plans for changing the regulatory mechanism but still maintaining CAB power within the same general framework. They usually involve elimination of the subsidy element (in any one of various ways) and putting all mail pay on a purely "service" basis. The larger and stronger trunklines also support this view. It has been suggested by one (large) carrier that trunks should be ineligible for subsidy. Cf. various statements of C. R. Smith, President of American Airlines, e.g., *The New York Times*, May 8, 1960, p. S–13; *Aviation Week*, May 9, 1960, p. 41. In mid-1961, Senator Warren G. Magnuson (Democrat, Washington) introduced legislation, drafted by the CAB, to make all domestic trunklines ineligible to receive subsidy. See *Aviation Week*, July 31, 1961, p. 42.

[12] See Appendix A.

[13] E. P. Warner, *The Early History of Air Transportation* (York: The Maple Press, 1938), p. 4.

and finally to the West Coast. By 1926, sufficient beacons had been installed so that the complete transcontinental airway was suitable for night flying.[14] These were outstanding advances in the commercial utilization of aircraft, and the government, through the Post Office Department, played an important role in this early development.

In 1925 Congress passed the Air Mail Act[15] (Kelly Act, after its originator, Congressman Clyde Kelly of Pennsylvania). This Act opened the door for the flying of mail by private carriers, with whom the Postmaster General was authorized to deal on the basis of submitted bids for specific routes.[16] The Air Commerce Act of 1926[17] assigned the responsibility for ground facilities along the air routes to the Department of Commerce. Thus the government continued to exercise important functions even after the actual business of moving the mail was transferred to private hands. The Air Commerce Act was also concerned with general issues regarding the proper role of the federal government in the development of civil air transportation.

A third amendment to the Kelly Act, known as the Watres Act, was passed in 1930.[18] It was important for at least two reasons. It specifically stipulated that all carriers providing air-mail service *must* also provide accommodation for passengers. Most of all the mail lines had made no particular provisions prior to the Act. If space was available between mail bags, it could be used by passengers; more formal arrangements did not exist. The Watres Act also authorized the Postmaster General to consolidate and extend the routes then existing, with an eye toward unifying the air transport industry and establishing a more adequate domestic system. This was done largely by awarding new contracts without the process of competitive bidding and by granting large extensions of existing routes to the carriers then operating.

The Democratic administration in 1934 charged the officials of the Post Office Department with fraud and collusion in their dealings with the lines carrying the mail. All contracts were subsequently canceled, and, after a particularly unsuccessful return engagement by the Army

[14] Joseph L. Nicholson, *Air Transportation Management* (New York: John Wiley & Sons, Inc., 1951), p. 12.

[15] 43 *Stat.* 805 (1925).

[16] The original Kelly Act and its first two amendments (1926 and 1928) had important provisions regarding the payment to be made to the carriers for the transport of mail, but these are not important for present purposes. The reader is again referred to Nicholson, *op. cit.*, pp. 14 ff.

[17] 44 *Stat.* 568 (1926).

[18] 46 *Stat.* 259 (1930).

Air Corps, the Air Mail Act of 1934 was passed.[19] This Act restored competitive bidding for specific routes; it also added an element of confusion through division of the authority that it established. The Post Office Department, in the person of the Postmaster General, continued to award route contracts on a limited term basis. The Interstate Commerce Commission was given the responsibility of examining the rates each year, with power to adjust wherever a carrier seemed to be earning unreasonable profits. The Department of Commerce continued to handle maintenance of ground facilities along the federal airways. Authority was clearly not unified, and there was a conspicuous lack of broad guiding principles.

The Civil Aeronautics Act of 1938

The Civil Aeronautics Act of 1938[20] set up one agency in place of the tripartite division under the 1934 legislation, but the agency still had three distinct bodies. This was an attempt at demarcation between executive, legislative, and judicial functions. The Civil Aeronautics Authority concerned itself with economic and safety regulations. An Administrator was appointed to exercise executive functions in the development of air navigation facilities. Finally, an Air Safety Board was established to investigate accidents.

In 1940 President Roosevelt transmitted Reorganization Plans 3 and 4 to his Congress, and they subsequently became effective.[21] An immediate, although minor, objection to these plans was the resulting confusion of terminology. The former Administrator of the Authority became Administrator, Civil Aeronautics Administration, and his duties were expanded to include the safety regulation formerly in the hands of the Authority. The Authority, however, whose name was changed to the Civil Aeronautics Board, continued economic regulation and also had the power to prescribe safety regulations. The former Air Safety Board became a branch of the Civil Aeronautics Board, with the title Bureau of Safety Regulation. Furthermore, the entire structure was brought back under the Department of Commerce (ostensibly for budgetary purposes), except that the Civil Aeronautics Board was to continue its functions independently for all practical purposes, reporting directly to Congress. It is within this framework

[19] 48 *Stat.* 933 (1934).
[20] 52 *Stat.* 977 (1938).
[21] 54 *Stat.* 1235 (1940).

that the Civil Aeronautics Authority and the Civil Aeronautics Board following it have considered problems of economic regulation.

The contents of the Act left little doubt that the government recognized a public interest in air transportation which extended beyond that of the postal service. The numerous points on which the extensive regulation of carrier economic activities was made specific need not be discussed here. It is of interest simply to note that broad power was now in the hands of a government body not only to regulate the postal business of the air carriers but also their increasingly important commercial business as well.

The statement of policy to which the Civil Aeronautics Board is committed in its decisions is of more relevance here:

> In the exercise and performance of its powers and duties under this Act, the Board shall consider the following, among other things, as being in the public interest, and in accordance with the public convenience and necessity —
>
> (a) The encouragement and development of an air-transportation system properly adapted to the present and future needs of the foreign and domestic commerce of the United States, of the Postal Service, and of the national defense;
>
> (b) The regulation of air transportation in such manner as to recognize and preserve the inherent advantages of, assure the highest degree of safety in, and foster sound economic conditions in such transportation, and to improve the relations between, and coordinate transportation by, air carriers;
>
> (c) The promotion of adequate, economical and efficient service by air carriers at reasonable charges, without unjust discriminations, undue preferences or advantages, or unfair or destructive competitive practices;
>
> (d) Competition to the extent necessary to assure the sound development of an air-transportation system properly adapted to the needs of the foreign and domestic commerce of the United States, of the Postal Service, and of the national defense;
>
> (e) The regulation of air commerce in such manner as to best promote its development and safety; and
>
> (f) The encouragement and development of civil aeronautics.[22]

The Civil Aeronautics Act provided in the so-called "Grandfather Clause"[23] that any established carrier who could show a record of

[22] 52 *Stat.* 977, 980 (1938); *Civil Aeronautics Act*, Section 2.
[23] 52 *Stat.* 987, Section 401 (e) (1).

continuous and satisfactory service from May 14, 1938, until August 22, 1938, should be granted the necessary permanent certificates for continued operation. Thus the Board did not begin with a clean map, as it were, but rather with a considerable number of airlines already in operation.[24]

This clause has often been cited as an explanation for the more recent route problems facing the CAB. That body inherited, it is argued, a hopeless and haphazard pattern without adequate power to change it. Some of the logic of this position is clear.[25] The original route pattern was based on air-mail contract routes awarded by the Post Office Department and was served typically with DC-2 and DC-3 aircraft with an economic range of less than 500 miles. For the four-engine aircraft types that came into commercial use by 1947, this range often exceeded 1,000 miles. Technological development implied much longer nonstop flight scheduling.

The amount of favor with which the Board has looked upon these original airlines shows considerable variation. The first case dealing with entry of a new carrier was decided in favor of the applicant.[26] Not long afterward another new company was allowed in the industry, this time primarily for air-mail carriage.[27] Thus the impression, both from the outcomes of these cases and also from the statements made in them,[28] is that carriers existing under the grandfather clause were not to be given any preference in new route development.

In less than a year, however, the Board formulated its "rule of exclusion," which was in conflict with the spirit of the above pronouncements.[29] This general point of view was in evidence

[24] Twenty-three carriers were awarded grandfather certificates in 1938.

[25] The question of the means to remedy the situation is not so clear. E.g., "The authority to award certificates for new service and to extend existing routes, provided the CAB with a powerful tool useful to alter the 'grandfather' route pattern in the interests of efficient service . . .," "Civil Aeronautics Board Policy: An Evaluation," 1073.

[26] *American Export Airlines, Certificate of Public Convenience and Necessity*, 2 CAB 16 (1940).

[27] *All American Aviation, Certificate of Public Convenience and Necessity*, 2 CAB 133 (1940).

[28] "Any such theory as advocated by the interveners, which would result in reserving solely for existing airlines the providing of all additions to the present air-transportation system of the United States, is untenable. Our adoption of such a policy would certainly not be consistent with a sound development of air transportation, and would not be conducive to the best interests of the foreign and domestic commerce of the United States, the Postal Service, and the national defense," *ibid.*, 146.

[29] "The number of air carriers now operating appears sufficient to insure against monopoly in respect to the average new route case, and we believe that the present

throughout the war period, but since that time a more liberal attitude seems to be in effect.

Carriers are to be issued certificates of public convenience and necessity when found fit, willing, and able to maintain a proposed operation in the public interest. These are elastic terms. Although the Act does nothing to define "fit, willing, and able," the Board has established the following tests:

1. A proper organizational basis for the conduct of air transportation.
2. A plan for the conduct of the service made by competent personnel.
3. Adequate financial resources.[30]

All of these items offer varying interpretations as well. The question of Board consistency in applying these rules will be discussed in more detail. The point of most interest here has been to show that since 1938 there has existed a relatively independent governmental agency acting within a detailed (but not unambiguous) legislative framework to guide and regulate the domestic air transportation industry.[31]

3. The Civil Aeronautics Board in Operation

Introduction

> . . . it is reasonably fair to say that the Congressional decision of 1938 amounted to a determination that a new agency of five men, vested with sweeping authority, should see to it that an infant transport industry, of more than passing importance to our military power, should be spared the evils of overbuilding, wasteful competitive warfare, bankruptcies,

---

domestic air-transportation system can by a proper supervision be integrated and expanded in a manner that will in general afford the competition necessary for the development of that system in the manner contemplated by the Act. In the absence of particular circumstances presenting an affirmative reason for a new carrier there appears to be no inherent desirability of increasing the present number of carriers merely for the purpose of numerically enlarging the industry," *Delta Air Corp., et al., Additional Service to Atlanta and Birmingham*, 2 CAB 447, 480 (1940).

[30] *Braniff Airways* v. *CAB*, 147 Fed (2d) 152, 153 (1945).

[31] The Federal Aviation Act of 1958, 72 *Stat.* 731 (1958), differs very little from its predecessor, the Civil Aeronautics Act of 1938, with respect to the concepts and methods of economic regulation that the CAB is to apply. Moreover, such examples as are relevant in the remainder of this study will be drawn from the record of CAB decisions in the two decades from the inception of detailed regulation in 1938. This is not because of any remarkable shift of policy after 1958, but rather because, at the time this study was undertaken, it was the last year for which there were adequate data.

rate discrimination, and business piracy which, in surface transportation, had concerned Congress for many years before it took remedial action. If any of these evils were to appear in the air as they had on earth it would be due to the faulty judgment of five men, not of Congress. That is just about the substance of the Civil Aeronautics Act.[32]

In this section Board decisions in selected cases will be examined to ascertain the extent to which there has been consistency in the weighing of factors bearing on new route cases. Of particular interest will be the determination of what sort of over-all route policy, if any, has been evolved and whether or not the efficiency of the route pattern has received adequate attention. The conclusion of this section is that although much emphasis has at various times been put on different portions of the Declaration of Policy, a consideration of the "promotion of adequate, economical, and efficient service by air carriers"[33] has been almost completely by-passed. It will be suggested later that a rigorous approach to the efficiency of the air service, when applied to route structure, would introduce a long overdue, unified approach to route pattern problems.

Discussion

The decisions of the CAB in its route cases have been subjected to criticism from many sides and on many grounds.[34] The Civil Aeronautics Act is complex and involved. It enumerates many considerations that the Board is to have in mind when deciding any of the

[32] Howard C. Westwood, "Choice of the Air Carrier for New Air Transport Routes," *George Washington Law Review*, XVI (December, 1947), 2.

[33] See p. 41, paragraph (c).

[34] It is tempting to generalize from evidence in specific areas to over-all errors in CAB policy. For example, with regard to the role of priority of filing in the choice among several carriers applying for a given route, one can trace a rather circular evolution of regulatory policy. In *Continental Air Lines, Inc., et al.—Mandatory Route*, 1 CAA 88 (1939), it is clearly stated that priority of application should not be a contributing factor influencing the choice of one from several carriers. By 1940, in *Braniff Airways, et al. — Houston-Memphis-Louisville Route*, 2 CAB 353 (1940), the Board's position was already easing, and by 1946, in *Rocky Mountain States Air Service*, 6 CAB 195 (1946), one reads that order of filing must be given some weight, when other considerations are equal. Furthermore, the Board has in at least one case denied an application because others for a similar or related service were pending, even though some of the latter were not filed until after the hearing on the application which was denied. See *Texas-Oklahoma Case*, 7 CAB 481 (1946).

One might argue that such action reflects either the lack of over-all, guiding policy on this point or else a lack of consistency in the application of enunciated standards. And then one might extend the argument to say that this is indicative of a general lack of consistency in Board action. But this would be an unfair conclusion, insofar as the

various kinds of cases with which it may be confronted. Under such a mandate, it is clear that no particular individual goal can be considered to the exclusion of all others. Nonetheless, one would expect an indication that the concept of efficiency for the over-all air route structure had received some attention over the years of CAB decisions.

Armed with this hope, an investigation of this question was undertaken: What evidence is there that the CAB has enunciated and followed a specific route policy (or set of policies) designed in some way to consider the over-all domestic route pattern and the adequacy, economy, and efficiency of such a structure and the service thereon? What does it understand by "efficiency" as it is expressed in Section 2 (c)[35] and also in Section 1002 (e) of the Civil Aeronautics Act; namely, that the Board should recognize

> the need in the public interest of adequate and efficient transportation of persons and property by air carriers at the lowest cost consistent with the furnishing of such service.[36]

Several early decisions seem to have been based on some consideration of relative costs involved. Insofar as the relative costs expected to be incurred by various carriers over a given route measure the "efficiency" of the operation (if only in an ordinal sense), the Board seems to have cleared its record both past and future when it declared

> In all new route cases much attention is devoted to the comparative costs which the applicants expect to incur in the development of the new service. Of course, it is essential to an economically sound enterprise that costs be kept at the lowest minimum consonant with adequate and efficient service. However, immediate costs are not necessarily controlling, as in that event that factor might conflict with other important statutory objectives.[37]

CAB should be allowed to evolve policy standards and approaches to difficult questions. The question of how much "evolution" is defensible is of course difficult. One of the intents of the Civil Aeronautics Act was to add an element of stability to an industry in which it was lacking. This should imply also enough stability of regulatory policy to allow firms directly affected to formulate their own longer-run plans on the basis of enunciated decisions and the underlying discussion that enumerates factors considered relevant by the regulatory authority. That this has not been the case is seen in the following: "At present, management must play the unrewarding game of second-guessing the Board, with the inevitable consequence that fear of a wrong guess stymies initiative and progress," or, ". . . the Board itself has been somewhat less than perfectly consistent in developing a basic regulatory policy or philosophy for the airline industry," United Research Incorporated, *op. cit.*, pp. vii and 21, respectively.

[35] See, p. 41.

[36] 52 *Stat.* 977, 1019 (1938).

[37] *Latin American Air Service,* 6 CAB 857, 900 (1946).

One writer has conducted an extensive survey of route award cases in early CAB history and finds that there are "relatively few instances where 'much attention' was paid to the comparative costs of the applicants competing for choice."[38]

In several early cases involving questions of parallel service authorization, the Board seemed to imply that the decisions were a result of actual comparison of the efficiency (in terms of comparative costs) of single vs. double carrier service. Keyes cites three cases in which

> ... the Board appears to have decided against the institution of competitive services on the basis of a calculation, however imprecise, of the most efficient distribution of a given volume of traffic between firms.[39]

Moreover, a case from the same period indicates that the Board saw the relevance of this to the functioning of the whole system. Another 1943 decision discusses the fact that "revenue-cost" ratios are relevant

> ... not only because of the possibility of their effect on mail rates payable to ... carriers, but also from the standpoint of efficiency and economy as those matters affect the question of the economically sound and efficient air-transport system.[40]

However, after a thorough reading of cases following this pronouncement by the Board, Keyes concludes:

> Nevertheless, the Board has evidently declared itself to be prepared to approve competitive services where *some* increase in operating cost will be involved as compared with a one-carrier operation; which is to say not only that the determination of the competitive pattern is not based *solely* on considerations of maximum efficiency (as of a given stage of "technique"), but that such considerations are not necessarily of overriding importance even in cases where they point clearly to a particular decision.[41]

[38] Howard C. Westwood, "Procedure in New Route Cases Before the Civil Aeronautics Board," *Journal of Air Law and Commerce*, XIV (Summer, 1947), 68.

[39] Lucille S. Keyes, *Federal Control of Entry into Air Transportation* (Cambridge: Harvard University Press, 1951), p. 133. The cases are *Canadian Colonial Airways, Ltd., Permit to Foreign Air Carrier*, 3 CAB 59 (1941); *Caribbean Atlantic Airlines, Inc., Puerto Rican Operations*, 3 CAB 717 (1942); *Pan American Airways, Inc., et al., Service from New Orleans to Cuba and Central America*, 4 CAB 161 (1943).

[40] *Eastern Air Lines, Inc., et al., Additional Washington Service*, 4 CAB 325, 335 (1943).

[41] Keyes, *op. cit.*, p. 127. Further, as Westwood points out: "... the Board spoke only of avoiding an *increase* in costs, without mention of the desirability of achieving a lower level of costs. The fact is that the Board's opinions betray virtually no thought of future cost trends," *Journal of Air Law and Commerce*, *op. cit.*, 227.

Two broad considerations seem to have been cited more often. Decisions against additional service were much more typically based on (1) the contention that existing traffic was not great enough to warrant additional service or (2) the argument that traffic diversion from existing operations would be too great. While these criteria are not patently incompatible with attainment of maximum efficiency, neither do they suggest specific consideration of that end.

Vigorous criticism came occasionally from within the Board itself. In 1944 Board member Lee dissented in a case involving route changes. He charged that the majority decision completely disregarded the mandates of the Declaration of Policy of Section 2, especially with respect to a long-range view of the route pattern that would promote and develop an integrated system of air transportation. Regarding the word "system" he wrote:

> The implication of the word goes further and includes the idea not only of a large overall pattern, but also of a pattern based on principle, a design into which the parts are fitted and not thrown haphazardly.[42]

This was a portent. In the years immediately following the conclusion of World War II, the Board approved a large number of new or duplicating route services. In a general way there appeared to be justification for such action. The war had focused attention on the airplane and made the public much more aware of flying. The existence of priority wartime demands on the few available civilian aircraft made air travel impossible for the average citizen. There was also the prospect of generally freer spending when the patriotic pressures for saving were removed or eased.

The CAB adopted and followed a policy of granting new route certificates, extending existing routes and amending certificates to provide for more nonstop schedules during the period 1945–1947. It should be remembered that this was being done at precisely the time when the airlines were initially supplementing their basic twin-engine DC-3 fleets with converted military DC-4 aircraft and later taking delivery of even-larger capacity, longer-range DC-6's, Constellations, and Boeing Stratocruisers. It has been estimated that such equipment changes alone, without any route extensions or authorizations from the Board, would have probably more than

[42] *Western Air Lines, Acquisition of Inland Airlines*, 4 CAB 654, 665 (1944).

doubled the amount of air transportation service offered to the public.[43]

A number of very searching investigations of the Board's route policy were made by government agencies as a result of the 1946–1948 authorizations. The reports of their findings hark back to Lee's dissent some five years earlier. In their 1949 study of national transportation policy, Dearing and Owen draw some sharp conclusions regarding the CAB's record:

> . . . we must conclude that administration of the Civil Aeronautics Act by the CAB has produced only one affirmative result. It has underwritten and accelerated expansion of the industry's route coverage and operating capacity. But it must be emphasized that the primary purpose of the act was to guide this development into a balanced and orderly operating pattern and to maintain sound economic conditions in the industry, presumably with a view to minimizing the amount of public subsidy required for its support.
>
> . . . the CAB has not succeeded in preventing the development of excessive air transport capacity, nor has it evolved a balanced corporate and operating structure for the industry.[44]

At the same time, a number of articles on the problem of lack of an over-all route structure began to appear in certain journals, especially in the *Journal of Air Law and Commerce*.[45] The response of the Board to these criticisms has not been impressive.[46]

[43] Goodrick, *op. cit.*, p. 289. This brings up the question of the Board's control over the amount of service on a route, once a carrier has been certificated to fly it, which is discussed on p. 49.

[44] Charles L. Dearing and Wilfred Owen, *National Transportation Policy* (Washington: The Brookings Institution, 1949), pp. 209–210. See also President's Air Policy Commission, *Survival in the Air Age* (Washington, D. C.: U.S. Government Printing Office, 1948), pp. 110–111.

[45] The most important of these are, in chronological order: Westwood, *op. cit.*; James M. Landis, "Air Routes Under the Civil Aeronautics Act," *Journal of Air Law and Commerce*, XV (Summer, 1948), 295–302; J. J. O'Connell, Jr., "Legal Problems in Revising the Air Route Pattern," *Journal of Air Law and Commerce*, XV (Autumn, 1948), 397–408; Louis E. Black, Jr., "Realignment of the Domestic Route Pattern," *Journal of Air Law and Commerce*, XV and XVI (Autumn, 1948), 409–433, and (Winter, 1949), 20–39; Adams, *op. cit.*; Goodrick, *op. cit.*; Harold D. Koontz, "Domestic Airline Self-Sufficiency: A Problem of Route Structure," *American Economic Review*, XLII (March, 1952), 103–125; and Paul D. Zook, "Recasting the Air Route Pattern by Airline Consolidations and Mergers," *Journal of Air Law and Commerce*, XXI (Summer, 1954), 293–311.

[46] Cf. Frederick, *op. cit.*, p. 202, note 13: "The Board has so far shown little real enthusiasm for, or fundamental appreciation of, the need for making the studies recommended (in 1948), stressing the difficulty in separating over-all planning of route development from its other functions."

This is all the more serious because of the essentially only permissive nature of the Board's powers. Mistakes or errors of judgment are not easily rectified. It can approve or disapprove the proposals submitted by carriers; it cannot order performance of any new service. Furthermore, once authorized to serve a route, the carrier enjoys almost complete freedom in choice of schedules and times to provide flights.[47] A certain amount of pressure is possible through the Post Office Department as far as provision for the mail flights is concerned, but this seems to have been a relatively minor constraint on the airlines in the past.[48]

It also appears that the CAB has or at least uses very little authority to correct situations where service has deteriorated or a decision may have been the result of poor judgment.[49] This is based both on statutory provision and historical record. The Civil Aeronautics Act provides that the Board may "alter, amend, modify or suspend" a carrier's certificate "if public convenience and necessity require" but then goes on to limit such revocations to instances where there was "... intentional failure to comply with any provision of Title IV of the Act ... or any order, rule or regulation issued thereunder, or any term, condition or limitation of such certificates."[50] A Supreme Court decision in 1946 made it clear that a certificate of convenience and necessity cannot be revoked in the absence of statutory authority.[51] The Board itself stated, in 1947, that it was not aware of legal means of transferring a carrier's property, business, or certificate to another carrier.[52]

The thorough work of Keyes terminated with 1951. On the basis of investigation of cases before that date, she concludes:

[47] 52 *Stat.* 977, 988–989 (1938); *Civil Aeronautics Act*, Section 401 (f). This was the interpretation that held since 1938. In 1960, however, the Board ordered that additional flights be scheduled between particular points and by a specific carrier. This is unprecedented. It has been upheld in the lower courts and will be examined by the Supreme Court. See *Aviation Week*, June 20, 1960, p. 91, July 18, 1960, p. 43 and January 9, 1961, p. 40.

[48] 52 *Stat.* 977, 985–990 (1938); *Civil Aeronautics Act*, Sections 405 (e), 401 (m). See also Keyes, *op. cit.*, p. 302: "Although the Board has power to require the furnishing of 'adequate' service, this phrase is usually construed to mean a minimum of performance, and probably could not be relied on to sanction more than a very small degree of initiative on the part of the Board in the adjustment of the quantity of service."

[49] Compare Frederick, *op. cit.*, p. 196 with D. Philip Locklin, *Economics of Transportation* (4th ed.; Homewood: Richard D. Irwin, Inc., 1954), p. 836.

[50] 52 *Stat.* 977, 989 (1938); *Civil Aeronautics Act*, Section 401 (h). Title IV covers Air Carrier Economic Regulation.

[51] *United States* v. *Seatrain Lines*, 329 U.S. 424 (1946).

[52] *United Air Lines, Inc., Acquisition of Air Carrier Property*, 8 CAB 298, 323 (1947).

> The specific powers over air transport granted to the CAB were apparently aimed at, and are probably adequate for, the achievement of the protection of particular firms; they were not aimed at, nor are they adequate for, the achievement of maximum efficiency in terms of economic performance.[53]

This apparent lack of legal authority to rectify ill-advised decisions leads one to the conclusion that an over-all, consistent policy is necessary. Further support for this position comes from the contention that long-run consistency is all the more difficult to achieve in a regulatory body whose composition changes frequently and erratically.

> The CAB must not be considered as a constant group of men in constant agreement on one constant answer. Rather, the Board has been characterized by an unusually high turnover of members and chairmen. This fluidity has necessarily been matched by a degree of corresponding fluidity of decisions. One Board may compromise on decisions favoring maximum competition, another may frown on this.[54]

To close this section, the *New York-Florida Case* will again be examined.[55] That case includes points which bear on the question of whether or not to authorize an additional carrier over a specific route. It also considers the question of which carrier to select, once the former decision has been made. Interest here is more intimately connected with the first of these two problems.

The case for inclusion of another carrier on the New York-Florida route rests heavily on the assertion that there is considerable passenger inconvenience during the prime winter season on this route. The Board argues that the two carriers which were providing service at the time of the case had vigorously competed in the market and brought to it many of the benefits of such competition.[56] Apparently these were not enough. Immediately at least two points come to mind: (1) Why would not an equipment pooling arrangement between the two airlines be an equally satisfactory and less wasteful way to handle an extremely seasonal route? (2) Do the benefits of effective competition

[53] Keyes, *op. cit.*, p. 330.

[54] Adams, *op. cit.*, p. 472.

[55] 24 CAB 94 (1956).

[56] *Ibid.*, p. 99. The Board then minimizes the importance to "the man in the street" of the difference between serving New York-Florida points with DC-6B or DC-7 aircraft (*ibid.*, p. 103). Yet such service improvements are precisely what the CAB says it is encouraging when it adds new competitors to a given route.

of a second carrier on a route eventually die out, so that then a third and perhaps later a fourth and more competitors are necessary to ensure that such benefits continue?

Arrangements such as pooling do not receive discussion because much of the argument in this case turns on the records of Eastern and National, the two lines already serving the routes. It is early established that "... the needs of the traveling public for service between the Northeast and Florida cities are not now being fully met by Eastern and National. ..."[57] Despite praise for the competitive spirit which has been maintained on the routes, the Board argues that reequipment programs and plans for increased services by these two airlines are not enough. There is little quantitative evidence regarding the ability of the carriers to handle projected traffic.

Light is shed on the second point by several statements which emphasize that another carrier should be authorized to develop the traffic potential of the markets concerned; and that if a third carrier seems unjustified on the basis of traffic current at the time of the hearing, it will be justified in the future by the growth in traffic which will accompany the new policies of another carrier.[58] Applicant airlines assert in testimony that the presence of load factors on the existing airlines of between 70 and 90 per cent indicates "inability to cope with public demand."[59] The Board does not make clear its position with regard to this evidence, but no objection seems to be raised. To condemn an airline because it has refrained from overscheduling its equipment is to ignore or misconstrue the meaning of efficiency on the particular route.

Examination of almost twenty years of decisions similar to the *New York-Florida Case* convinced another recent student of CAB policy that efficiency was being badly ignored.

> In the course of its decisions and in the promulgation of policy, the CAB should also give evidence that it has at least considered the impact of its actions upon firm and industry "efficiency" in some sense. ... Put the most simply, the question might be the degree to

[57] *Ibid.*, p. 99.

[58] *Ibid.*, pp. 101, 197.

[59] *Ibid.*, p. 174. Apparently this view is common in the industry. Cf. Frederick, *op. cit.*, p. 96 and Samuel B. Richmond, *Regulation and Competition in Air Transportation* (New York: Columbia University Press, 1961), pp. 111 ff. Richmond's thorough study became available too late to be noted in detail. It is an excellent analysis and discussion of many of the questions that have been only touched upon in this chapter.

which strengthening (i.e., improving the "efficiency" of) the smaller trunk carriers is being achieved at the cost of imposing a "diseconomy" upon carriers already in the market. To be sure, it is not necessary that the Board always operate so as to improve the efficiency of the industry in the short run. However, there would seem to be a heavy burden upon the Board to make clear just how any decision which does not promote maximum efficiency in the air transport industry in the short run does result in the optimum and orderly development of the air transport system of the United States in the long run.[60]

Conclusions

The CAB decisions presented in the preceding section have been reviewed previously by other investigators who were interested in facets of regulatory policy. Some have found an over-all consistency in Board action, but this has been at the cost of suppressing particular details. Others have found no apparent guiding policy in route awards. Clearly, lack of consistent action could be the result of either the nonexistence of over-all policy guides or a lack of consistency by the Board in applying what principles did exist; or it could be a combination of the two. It seems that the former is closer to the truth. There simply was and is no articulate route policy, despite the fact that the Board has been hearing cases for over twenty years under the same set of economic regulations. Moreover, the particular term "efficiency" has received little if any explicit consideration and certainly no emphasis in Board decisions.

These points suggest the usefulness of a method that would give operational meaning to efficiency in the structure of air routes and thus be applicable in a variety of cases. While not necessarily of interest for all CAB decisions, such a method would certainly be useful in those cases where efficiency *is* a relevant factor. Then, too, management would know better what to expect, once efficiency had been cited as important in a decision. If efficiency as a policy consideration has been superseded by other goals, the method presented here could still be relevant at some future date, should the notion of efficiency assume more importance.

Furthermore, the method has much more general application as a

[60] Aaron J. Gellman, "The Regulation of Competition in United States Domestic Air Transportation: A Judicial Survey and Analysis," *Journal of Air Law and Commerce*, XXIV (Autumn, 1957, and Spring, 1958), 181.

supplement to other types of analysis in industry studies. Its application here might be looked upon as an example of such use as well. As an inquiry into the performance of an industry and specifically into the particular dollar costs of nonoptimal allocation of capacity, regardless of regulatory overtones, the remainder of this study should be of interest. The next two chapters detail the model proposed for these purposes.

Chapter 4

The Model: Basic Formulation

IT IS THE AIM AND FUNCTION of this chapter to present the underlying logic and the mathematical models that will be used to analyze a segment of the domestic trunk airline industry. The result will be a framework that should provide the quantitative basis for comments on the efficiency of that industry. Conclusions will rest heavily on the abstract representation derived here as well as on the accuracy of the data used.

Section 1 discusses linear programming models and the usefulness of such methods for the particular interests of this investigation. Section 2 provides the notation which is necessary for the development of Section 3, the models. Section 4 is devoted to the concept and relevance of integer programming and its relationship to transhipment possibilities. In Section 5 the work of the chapter is summarized. Appendix B indicates directions in which the model might be extended.

1. Linear Programming, Regulation, and Efficiency

An extensive literature now exists on linear programming, covering both the theoretical foundations and applications.[1] It is, in general

[1] The following, among others, are good references: R. G. D. Allen, *Mathematical Economics* (London: Macmillan & Co., Ltd., 1956); A. Charnes, W. W. Cooper and A. Henderson, *An Introduction to Linear Programming* (New York: John Wiley & Sons, Inc., 1953); R. Dorfman, P. A. Samuelson, and R. Solow, *Linear Programming and Economic Analysis* (New York: McGraw-Hill Book Company, Inc., 1958); T. C. Koopmans (ed.), *Activity Analysis of Production and Allocation* (New York: John Wiley & Sons, Inc., 1951); S. Vajda, *The Theory of Games and Linear Programming*

terms, a means of solving maximization or minimization problems in which some or all of the variables are under the influence of constraints. That is, variables entering into the general function (the "objective function") which is to be maximized or minimized also may appear in one or more additional equations or inequalities which are interpreted as restraints on the system.

The familiar problem of enclosing a maximum rectangular area with a given amount of fencing may be considered a programming problem (nonlinear). The objective is to maximize area (= length × width) subject to the condition that twice the length plus twice the width may not exceed the total amount of fencing material available. Formally, this could be stated as:

$$\text{Maximize: } A = lw$$

$$\text{Subject to: } 2l + 2w \leq c$$

Other techniques may also be applied to such relatively simple problems, of course; it is with more complex situations that linear programming is chiefly concerned.

In the general case there is a linear function of several or many

(New York: John Wiley & Sons, Inc., 1956); S. Vajda, *Readings in Linear Programming* (New York: John Wiley & Sons, Inc., 1958); and Saul I. Gass, *Linear Programming: Methods and Applications* (New York: McGraw-Hill Book Company, Inc., 1958). For interregional linear programming theory, see Walter Isard, "Interregional Linear Programming: An Elementary Presentation and a General Model," *Journal of Regional Science*, I (Summer, 1958), 1–59; Benjamin H. Stevens, "An Interregional Linear Programming Model," *Journal of Regional Science*, I (Summer, 1958), 60–98; and also Benjamin H. Stevens, "A Review of the Literature on Linear Methods and Models for Spatial Analysis," *Journal of the American Institute of Planners*, XXVI (August, 1960), 253–259; Benjamin H. Stevens and R. E. Coughlin, "A Note of Inter-Areal Linear Programming for a Metropolitan Region," *Journal of Regional Science*, I (Spring, 1959) 75–83. Applied studies in this area include: K. A. Fox, "A Spatial Equilibrium Model of the Livestock-Feed Economy in the United States," *Econometrica*, XXI (October, 1953), 547–566; K. A. Fox and R. C. Taeuber, "Spatial Equilibrium Models of the Livestock Feed Economy," *American Economic Review*, XLV (September, 1955), 584–608; James M. Henderson, *The Efficiency of the Coal Industry* (Cambridge: Harvard University Press, 1959); James M. Henderson, "The Utilization of Agricultural Land: A Regional Approach," *Review of Economics and Statistics*, XLI (August, 1959), 242–259; G. G. Judge, "Competition Position of the Connecticut Poultry Industry — 7. A Spatial Equilibrium Model for Eggs," Bulletin 318, Storrs Agricultural Experiment Station, University of Connecticut, January, 1956; A Koch and M. Snodgrass, "Linear Programming Applied to Location and Product Flow Determination in the Tomato Processing Industry," *Papers and Proceedings of the Regional Science Association*, Vol. 5, 1959, pp. 151–162; and M. Snodgrass and C. E. French, *Linear Programming Approach to Interregional Competition in Dairying*, Agricultural Experiment Station, Purdue University, 1958.

variables which is to be maximized or minimized, subject to the conditions imposed by a set of linear restraints.

Maximize:

$$a_1x_1 + a_2x_2 + \cdots + a_nx_n$$

Subject to:

$$\begin{array}{ccccccc} b_{11}x_1 & + & b_{12}x_2 & + \cdots + & b_{1n}x_n & \leq & c_1 \\ b_{21}x_1 & + & b_{22}x_2 & + \cdots + & b_{2n}x_n & \leq & c_2 \\ \vdots & & \vdots & & \vdots & & \vdots \\ b_{m1}x_1 & + & b_{m2}x_2 & + \cdots + & b_{mn}x_n & \leq & c_m \end{array}$$

where many of the b's may be zero (i.e., not all variables need enter into all constraints). This sort of formulation may represent a situation in which a firm is trying to maximize total profit on several production items (x's), where per-unit profits are indicated by the a's. The constraints may indicate resource availabilities or capacity limitations, where the c's are maximum amounts of resource or capacity available and the b's are per-unit input requirements for the production of each product x. Typical minimization problems are ones in which total cost is to be minimized subject to the conditions that certain basic requirements or demands must be met, removing the possibility that all variables become zero (or negative). A correct formulation of a cost minimization allocation problem will meet the constraints and stated requirements at less expense than any other permissible allocation (or at an equal expense). In this sense it will provide an efficient allocation of activities.

Management has become much interested in linear programming and various associated techniques, all of which are extremely relevant to present-day business problems. In the current study, it is hoped that the model employed accurately embodies the constraints which are most important in the air transportation industry and that the objective of minimizing total direct operating costs is a reasonable and realistic one. The formulation used might serve as a basis for studies by individual airlines to whom cost savings should be of interest.

Regardless of whether or not the individual carriers may be relied upon to make their own particular decisions optimally, the total allocation may be inefficient from the interfirm point of view. It is the contention of this writer that the language of Section 2 of the Civil Aeronautics Act may be interpreted and understood in this larger sense; the legal emphasis is on an air transportation system or network.

Thus a linear programming model for the allocation of flights of given types of aircraft along particular routes will be formulated. These routes span the domestic United States; i.e., they transcend particular airline boundaries. The object will be to meet passenger demand at least cost. Cargo or freight movements will not be included in the model, although extensions in these directions would be possible. A network of domestic airports (nodes) will be selected. The computational complexities of the problem make it necessary to select a relatively small number of important passenger-generating areas.[2] Given the available stock of aircraft owned by the domestic trunklines serving the nodes selected, given direct costs and other operating characteristics of each aircraft type between each possible pair of nodes, and given passenger demand, it is possible to formulate a linear program to distribute this demand among available aircraft in such a manner as to minimize total direct operating costs while meeting a series of availability constraints, balance equations, and demand requirements.

2. Notation

For the remainder of this study the following notation will be employed.[3] Superscripts J, K, and L will refer to origins or destinations, i.e., they are locations; subscript h will refer to type of aircraft; r will denote the load factor, expressed as a per cent of capacity. The unknowns (all with reference to the time period selected for analysis) are

${}_{r}^{J}x_{h}^{K}$ number of nonstop flights of type h aircraft scheduled to fly from J to K with a load factor r

[2] At the time that the data were being collected for this study, it was planned to use a Control Data Corporation CDC–1604 computer. This machine has a core memory of 32,768 words of 48 bits each, and after allowing for the Simplex Routine program itself and allocating an adequate number of storage cells, around 25,000 cells were available for the matrix. This put strict limits on the permissible combinations of numbers of nodes and number of aircraft types that might be considered. In the final stages, however, a different machine was used (IBM 7090), and larger problems could have been handled.

[3] This notation is standard for interregional models. See Walter Isard, *Methods of Regional Analysis: an Introduction to Regional Science* (New York: The Technology Press of M.I.T. and John Wiley & Sons, Inc., 1960), esp. pp. 451–460.

${}^{J}y^{KL}$ number of *passengers* moved from J to K as an intermediate point on the way to L, their ultimate destination

${}^{J}d^{K}$ unsatisfied passenger demand for transportation from J to K

The relevant parameters are

${}^{J}_{r}a^{K}_{h}$ number of passengers that could be carried on plane type h over the route from J to K with a load factor r. Thus, ${}^{J}_{r}a^{K}_{n} = (r)({}^{J}V^{K}_{h})$, where ${}^{J}V^{K}_{h}$ is total seating capacity of plane type h over the route from J to K

${}^{J}b^{K}_{h}$ number of hours necessary from airplane type h to fly from J to K

${}^{J}_{r}c^{K}_{h}$ direct operating cost per trip for plane type h over route from J to K

S_h total available hours of aircraft type h

${}^{J}D^{K}$ passenger demand for air transportation from J to K

${}^{J}p^{K}$ price of a ticket from J to K

In a complete model most of these symbols might have a further designation for either first-class, coach-class, or combined service.

3. Models

Basic Formulation

The working basis for the remainder of the study is set forth in this section. By the systematic compounding of more assumptions into the basic structure, a so-called "master model" is developed. From this will come the "operational model" through consideration of factors discussed in the following chapter.[4]

What is desired is a model that will assign aircraft to the various routes under consideration in an economical and efficient way, depending upon the differing operating costs, carrying capabilities, and ranges of the available aircraft types, and the demands for

[4] Several less satisfactory models emerged during the logical development of this final formulation. In general they tended to be more cumbersome and also less complete than the one presented in the text.

transportation.[5] Optimal assignment will be understood to be that which can be carried out at least cost.

Employing the notation of Section 2, the following linear programming model is formulated:

$$\text{Minimize:} \quad \sum_J \sum_K \sum_h \sum_r {}^J_r c^K_h \, {}^J_r x^K_h + \sum_J \sum_K {}^J p^K \, {}^J d^K$$

Subject to:

$$1. \quad \sum_K {}^J y^{KL} - \sum_K {}^K y^{JL} + {}^J d^L = {}^J D^L \qquad (J \neq K)^6$$

$$2. \quad \sum_K \sum_r {}^K_r x^J_h - \sum_K \sum_r {}^J_r x^K_h \geq 0 \qquad (J \neq K)$$

$$3. \quad -\sum_J \sum_K \sum_r {}^J b^K_h \, {}^J_r x^K_h \geq - S_h \qquad (J \neq K)$$

[5] The following references contain models (of ostensibly similar interest) that have come to this writer's attention: A. R. Ferguson and G. B. Dantzig, "The Problem of Routing Aircraft," *Aeronautical Engineering Review*, XIV (April, 1955), 51–55; A. R. Ferguson and G. B. Dantzig, "The Allocation of Aircraft to Routes — An Example of Linear Programming Under Uncertain Demand," *Management Science*, III (October, 1956), 45–73; H. Markowitz and A. S. Manne, "On the Solution of Discrete Programming Problems," *Econometrica*, XXV (January, 1957), 84–110; A. S. Manne, "Air Cargo Transport Scheduling — An Illustrative Block Triangular System," Rand Corporation Paper P–533, June 11, 1954; S. Vajda, *Readings in Linear Programming*, Chapter 12, "Routing Aircraft," Herman W. von Guerard, *An Economic Model for Assigning Passenger Airplane Flights* (Burbank: Lockheed Aircraft Corp., 1959); A. C. Broman, M. Arbarbi, and M. D. Dawson, "A Mathematical Approach to the Routing of Aircraft," Market Research Report, Sales and Contracts Department, Transport Division, Boeing Airplane Company, Renton, Washington, 1958; Joseph F. McCloskey and Fred Hanssmann, "An Analysis of Stewardess Requirements and Scheduling for a Major Airline," *Naval Research Logistics Quarterly*, IV (September, 1957), 183–191; G. Morton, "Application of Linear Programming Methods to Commercial Airline Operations" (abstract), *Econometrica*, XXI (January, 1953), 193; T. E. Bartlett, "An Algorithm for the Minimum Number of Transport Units to Maintain a Fixed Schedule," *Naval Research Logistics Quarterly*, IV (June, 1957), 139–149; V. B. Gleaves, "Cyclic Scheduling and Combinatorial Topology: Assignment and Routing of Motive Power to Meet Scheduling and Maintenance Requirements. Part I — A Statement of the Operation Problem of the Frisco Railroad," *Naval Research Logistics Quarterly*, IV (September, 1957), 203–205; David L. Johnson, *Network Flow Theory and Its Application to Air Transport Problems* (Boeing Scientific Research Laboratories, Mathematical Note No. 218; Seattle: Boeing Airplane Company, 1960). In almost all cases the formulations were concerned with rather different objectives from those of this study. The papers by Manne and by Markowitz and Manne are most closely related to the present models.

[6] Following conventional notation, superscripts on the right side denote destinations. Therefore, in ${}^J y^{KL}$, $J = K$ would be meaningless. $J = L$ would be meaningless also. However, $K = L$ would indicate a direct shipment from J to L. For ${}^K y^{JL}$ terms, $J = K$ and $K = L$ are inadmissible for similar reasons; $J = L$ would denote a direct shipment from K to L.

$$4. \quad \sum_h \sum_r {}^J_r a^K_h \, {}^J_r x^K_h - \sum_L {}^J y^{KL} \geq 0 \qquad (J \neq K, L)$$

$$5. \quad \text{All } x, y, \text{ and } d \geq 0$$

The objective function seeks to minimize total cost, where this cost is made up of two elements: first, that originating in flying the various aircraft over different routes, and second, that which may be classed as lost revenue from untransported passengers.

The constraints have the following interpretations:

1. The first summation on the left indicates all outbound traffic from any individual node J destined for L, either directly (K may equal L) or via another node (or nodes) K. The second summation indicates all traffic coming into J, from all other nodes K, which is ultimately destined for L. The difference of these two summations will be the number of passengers who originate at node J and are destined for node L, by either a direct or an indirect routing. This difference must equal the demand at J for transportation to L, except for unfilled demand, which is the balancing item. Note that this formulation does not preclude the routing of traffic through more than one node. If there are U nodes, there will be at most $(U)(U - 1)$ such constraints.[7]

2. At each node, there are not more departures than arrivals of flights of any given aircraft type. Some piling up, of course, may

[7] Assume that four nodes exist. The constraints, for demands from nodes 1, 2, and 3, to go to node 4, would appear as follows:

$$\begin{aligned} {}^1y^{34} + {}^1y^{24} + {}^1y^{44} - {}^3y^{14} - {}^2y^{14} + {}^1d^4 &= {}^1D^4 \\ {}^2y^{34} + {}^2y^{14} + {}^2y^{44} - {}^3y^{24} - {}^1y^{24} + {}^2d^4 &= {}^2D^4 \\ {}^3y^{24} + {}^3y^{14} + {}^3y^{44} - {}^2y^{34} - {}^1y^{34} + {}^3d^4 &= {}^3D^4 \end{aligned}$$

Actual traffic out of node 1, which goes directly to its ultimate destination, node 4, includes all traffic that has passed through node 1 as the final intermediate point before 4. Conceptually, the activities within the period may be thought of in the following sequence: (1) Demands D are stated; (2) all indirect movements, ${}^Jy^{KL}$ $(K \neq L)$ are made; (3) all final movements, ${}^Jy^{KL}$ $(K = L)$ are made. Therefore, from the above,

$$({}^1D^4 - {}^1d^4) + ({}^2D^4 - {}^2d^4) + ({}^3D^4 - {}^3d^4) = {}^1y^{44} + {}^2y^{44} + {}^3y^{44}$$

That is, the number of passengers who arrive at node 4, from all other nodes, whose ultimate destination is node 4 equals the number of passengers sent from various origins to node 4 as destination. The constraint set 1 assures not only that the correct *numbers* of people arrive at each destination, but also that the correct *individuals* make up these numbers; i.e., it assures that any "transshipment" is carried out in the course of the period and no passengers are left stranded short of their goal.

occur.[8] If there are t airplane types, there will be at most $(U)(t)$ such constraints.

3. Total hours of use allocated to each airplane type must be less than or equal to total available hours for that type. The balancing item would be the nonnegative number of hours of use not assigned within the system being considered. There will be exactly t of these constraints. The signs have been reversed to preserve the desired direction of the inequality.

4. The total number of passengers moved over each route J to K will be accommodated by the total scheduled number of passenger transporting planes of all types on that segment.

5. A negative value for any of the unknowns would be meaningless, and is therefore not allowed.

4. The Role of an Integer or Discrete Programming Model

It is perhaps logical to consider including an integer requirement on the variables in the model. That is, the x's and y's should be constrained to whole numbers. This apparently simple addition to the programming problem is in fact one of far-reaching significance. There are many problems in which noninteger values are meaningless and rounding is not appropriate. Furthermore, rather different results may emerge when the same problem is treated in first a continuous and then a discrete formulation.

Until recently no rigorous method existed for solving such programs, and yet it was realized that a number of not uncommon situations might be represented by such a formulation.[9] No satisfactory meaning can be attached to 13.17 flights per week of a DC-7C from New York

[8] This is only one of several possible balance conditions. These constraints might include spare aircraft available at particular nodes and require that the net outflow from each node not exceed the number of spares at that point.

[9] Ralph Gomory must be credited with the first operational computational method for solving integer programs. His work is found in R. Gomory, "Outline of an Algorithm for Integer Solutions to linear Programs," *Bulletin of the American Mathematical Society*, LXIV (September, 1958), 275–278. Also see Markowitz and Manne, *op. cit.*, 84–110; A. H. Land and A. G. Doig, "An Automatic Method of Solving Discrete Programming Problems," *Econometrica*, XXVIII (July, 1960), 497–520; Ralph E. Gomory and William J. Baumol, "Integer Programming and Pricing," *Econometrica*, XXVIII (July, 1960), 521–550; William J. Baumol, *Economic Theory and Operations Analysis* (Englewood Cliffs: Prentice-Hall, Inc., 1961), esp. Chapter 6, "Nonlinear Programming," and Chapter 7, "Integer Programming."

to Chicago,[10] nor does shipment of 148.32 passengers via Cleveland satisfy the fastidious among us. But rounding is always available. The larger the values of the variables involved, the smaller the relative distortion, or error, and thus the less uncomfortable one may feel. However, there are some sorts of problems (notably the traveling-salesman problem) where numbers are used for enumeration of alternative geographic locations. It is meaningless to be told to proceed next to region 1.75, where integers have been used to designate areas of the country.[11]

If it were true that the only problem involved in using a continuous model were the conceptual one of fractional aircraft, discrete programs would not be necessary. The accuracy of available data does not warrant attaching significance to the decimals in a solution; rounding at least to the nearest whole number is called for. However, as will be shown by a more detailed example, the discrete model may give results that are structurally different from those of the continuous formulation; e.g., the former may allow transshipment where the latter does not.

Example 1

Consider a system with one type of equipment having a capacity of 100 passengers, with flying costs directly proportional to air distance. If a demand of 101 existed between two points, the continuous case would assign a value of 1.01 to ${}^Jx^K$ (number of flights from origin J to destination K); i.e., it would dispatch one complete airplane and a further 1/100th of a plane. The objective function would record an attendant cost of $1.01\,{}^Jc^K$, where ${}^Jc^K$ is the cost of flying the airplane from J to K.

Now introduce an intermediate node and assume the same equipment is available. The numbers indicate westbound demands. The

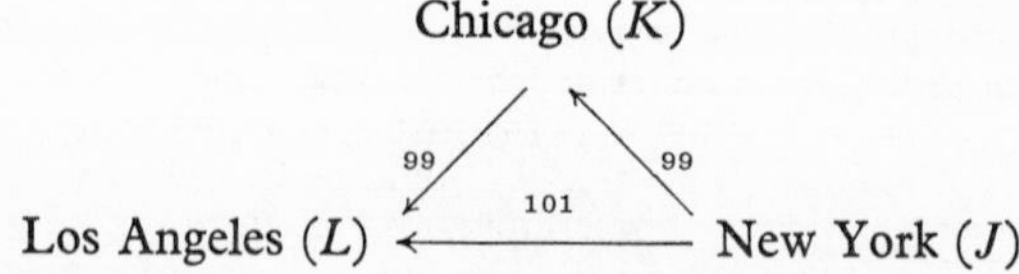

[10] Several writers have allowed fractional results and have interpreted them as representing flights scheduled over only part of the total time period or, alternatively, at wider intervals. See Ferguson and Dantzig, *Aeronautical Engineering Review*, *op. cit.*, 52; or S. Vajda, *Readings in Linear Programming*, p. 42.

[11] The number 1 may designate New England and 2 the Pacific Northwest.

routing of one passenger from New York to Los Angeles via Chicago would save the cost of flying an almost empty aircraft from New York to Los Angeles. A continuous model, relying on straightforward geometry, might compare total costs involved in both direct and indirect shipment of the 101st passenger. These would be $1.01^{J}c^{L} + 0.99^{J}c^{K} + 0.99^{K}c^{L}$ and $1.00^{J}c^{L} + 1.00^{J}c^{K} + 1.00^{K}c^{L}$, respectively. Since the former would be smaller, this passenger would be dispatched over the most direct route.[12] An integer model, however, would compare the direct routing total cost of $2^{J}c^{L} + {}^{J}c^{K} + {}^{K}c^{L}$ with the indirect routing cost ${}^{J}c^{L} + {}^{J}c^{K} + {}^{K}c^{L}$ and would select the transshipment route for the 101st passenger.[13] Thus the discrete formulation is able to cope with the air transport industry phenomenon that the cost of given aircraft flying a specific route is about the same regardless of the number of passengers.[14]

Theoretically, transshipment seems to be an important part of the model for passenger air travel. Actually, however, there are reasons why the transshipment feature of the formulation is not necessarily a predominant one:

1. Certain transshipment routes, although cheaper in terms of total cost, will be unacceptable from the point of view of the passenger. Available space on several connecting flights from A to B via a great number of widely dispersed intermediate nodes might be prohibitively time-consuming.[15]

[12] Since $0.01^{J}c^{L} < 0.01^{J}c^{K} + 0.01^{K}c^{L}$; i.e. $(0.01^{J}c^{L} - 0.01^{J}c^{K} + 0.01^{K}c^{L}) < 0$.

[13] This is the conclusion reached by Markowitz and Manne, *op. cit.*, 100. The importance of a discrete formulation for transport models is also discussed in R. Saposnik, V. L. Smith, and A. R. Lindeman, "Allocation of a Resource to Alternative Probabilistic Demands: Transport Equipment Pool Assignments," *Naval Research Logistics Quarterly*, VI (September, 1959), 193–207.

[14] Cf., for example, Russel E. Westmeyer, *Economics of Transportation* (New York: Prentice-Hall, Inc., 1952), p. 612; also John H. Frederick, *Commercial Air Transportation* (4th ed.; Homewood: Richard D. Irwin, 1955), p. 162.

[15] There appear to be at least three ways in which this problem could be treated; each is less elegant than the preceding one:

(*a*) Incorporate a predetermined limit on indirect routings. One could specify that the mileage covered may not exceed a given percentage of that on the most direct (i.e., nonstop) route. For example, assume that 20 per cent above the direct route mileage was taken as the maximum increase allowable with transshipment. Let ${}^{J}m^{K}$ = air mileage from J to K; then a new set of constraints would be called for which stated:

$$\text{If} \quad {}^{J}m^{K} + {}^{K}m^{L} > 1.2^{J}m^{L}, \quad \text{then} \quad {}^{J}y^{KL} = 0$$

Note that

$$\text{If} \quad {}^{J}m^{K} + {}^{K}m^{L} \leq 1.2^{J}m^{L}, \quad {}^{J}y^{KL} \text{ may or may not be zero.}$$

One might draw inspiration from Pythagoras and formulate the "Pythagorean (or

2. A frequently cited reason for including transshipment possibilities in a general transport model is the fact that a direct link from J to K may not exist, or that its capacity may be filled, and that it may be costly to construct additional facilities (i.e., railroad lines, lanes in a highway, etc.). These points are clearly less relevant here, where virtually every pair of nodes can be connected directly — at least up to the nonstop range of modern aircraft. There is, in effect, no additional cost in beginning direct service between two nodes, provided that terminal facilities are available at both ends (as indeed they will be in a model that considers existing domestic air traffic generating centers).[16]

It is of interest here to point out that the Orden modification of a regular transportation problem to take care of transshipment does not seem appropriate for the present analysis.[17] The regular transportation problem is concerned with the distribution of a single

---

Circular) Constraint," whereby any one-step deviation would be allowed if the intermediate node fell on or within the circle whose diameter was the straight line between the points J and L. This would read:

$$\text{If} \quad ({}^{J}m^{K})^2 + ({}^{K}m^{L})^2 > ({}^{J}m^{L})^2, \quad {}^{J}y^{KL} = 0$$

For more than one intermediate node, moreover, this neat geometry has an advantage. At each intermediate point there is again the choice of direct or indirect movement (it is this quality of the model which allows for several-stop movement between any two points). Whereas with the "20 Per Cent Constraint" it would be (theoretically) possible to move farther and farther away from the ultimate destination, this second proposal always shortens the distance through the elementary property of circles that a diameter is the longest possible chord. However, either method would do satisfactorily well for a model with a relatively small number of nodes, and both would eliminate a New York to Los Angeles routing via Miami, for example.

(*b*) For a small enough model, merely diagram the nodes and network on a map and then decide from the beginning which routings will not be acceptable, equating the corresponding ${}^{J}y^{KL}$ to zero.

(*c*) It is also possible to allow the model to ship via *any* routings, and to argue that, out of the total numbers of passengers handled, this would be a relatively small percentage. Furthermore, not all of the routings would be unsatisfactory, whereas allowing noninteger results (and thus avoiding false transshipments) solves the problem only by eliminating it, viz., by shipping directly but fractionally.

[16] There is one minor exception to this point. If direct service between two widely separated points introduces the need for larger, longer-range, aircraft, perhaps jets, it is conceivable that runways would require lengthening to accommodate the new equipment. It is suggested, however, that this is better thought of as an inevitable change necessitated by technological advancement in the industry. In addition, Professor Joseph Rose correctly points out that overcrowding of terminal facilities at busy airports might be treated as capacity constraints on certain arcs.

[17] Alex Orden, "The Transshipment Problem," *Management Science*, II (April 1956), 276–258. This is also discussed and applied in Richard E. Quandt, "Models of Transportation and Optimal Network Construction," *Journal of Regional Science*, II (Spring, 1960), 27–45.

product from several factory sites to various consumption centers; the object is to minimize total shipping cost. In general form:

Minimize: $$\sum_J \sum_K {}^J c^K \, {}^J x^K$$

Subject to:

$$1. \quad \sum_J {}^J x^L = b^K \quad (K = 1, \cdots, n)$$

$$2. \quad \sum_K {}^J x^K = {}^J a \quad (J = 1, \cdots, m)$$

And all ${}^J x^K \geq 0$

This is representative of the problem faced by a single-product firm, for example, with m production locations from which n different demand centers are to be satisfied. Individual plant capacities, ${}^J a$, are to be exhausted; demands at each center, b^K, are met exactly. Total amounts of product which can be produced at all plants, $\sum_{J=1}^{m} {}^J a$, and the total amount demanded at all consumption points, $\sum_{K=1}^{n} b^K$, are known and equal.

From this formulation, Orden is able to devise a clever scheme to allow transshipment by considering each node (in the preceding formulation either a producer or a consumer) as both a shipper and a receiver of the product. By further endowing each node with a fictitious stockpile of the product against which withdrawals and to which additions can be made, the model is made to encompass transshipments.

A second model for dealing with transshipment has been mentioned by Quandt, primarily as a logical step on the way to what is essentially the Orden formulation. This is a complete enumeration model which begins, as before, with the general form of the transportation model. As the name implies, this model keeps a complete account, for every pair of nodes, of all possible routings that a shipment may take between them. This leads to an exceptionally large number of possible activities.[18] This model is an interesting theoretical construct, but Quandt abandons it for a formulation similar to Orden's for any practical problem.

There seem to be important considerations in the model of air transport proposed for this study which make both of the preceding

[18] See Quandt, *op. cit.*, 35.

formulations awkward to apply. They issue most directly from the important feature of general transportation models that particular shippers are paired off with particular destinations only in the course of arriving at the optimal solution to the problem. Producers do not generally have prespecified preferences to whom they ship; in the same sense, consumers do not care from whom they buy. In the formulation of this study, although each point acts both as a consumer and as a producer, all demands are directed. It does not seem helpful to consider aggregates such as F_i, the sum of all demands out of node i, and T_j, the total of all demands to go to node j. In an aggregate formulation such as the general transportation model, where each point can be both a shipper and a receiver, if demand at two nodes were equal, and both were also producers, it is not likely that shipments would occur between the two; the two figures would cancel each other.[19] Each point would supply itself first, wherever this was possible. But in this study, 200 passengers demanding transportation from Boston to New York and 200 persons in New York wanting transportation to Boston must not cancel out.

For these reasons, the more cumbersome model of Section 3 was devised. It is an additional interesting feature of this model that although it allows for transshipment in its general formulation, it is only by virtue of the integer requirement on the x variables that transshipment is allowed to occur. This is what the Example 1 illustrated. It is now shown further.

Example 2

Assume three nodes, J, K, and L, and one model aircraft with a capacity of 100 persons. Assume demands and costs as follows:

Demands:	${}^{J}D^{K} = 90$	${}^{K}D^{J} = 100$
	${}^{K}D^{L} = 90$	${}^{L}D^{K} = 100$
	${}^{J}D^{L} = 110$	${}^{L}D^{J} = 100$
Costs:	${}^{J}C^{K} = 40$	${}^{K}C^{J} = 40$
	${}^{K}C^{L} = 70$	${}^{L}C^{K} = 70$
	${}^{J}C^{L} = 90$	${}^{L}C^{J} = 90$

A solution to the continuous problem was found after six iterations.[20]

[19] In general, only the net difference between any two nodes would be shipped, except when production capacity is exhausted at one or more nodes.

[20] See William J. Baumol, *op. cit.*, pp. 76–88, for an explanation of the straightforward procedure.

The results were as follows:

$$
\begin{array}{llll}
{}^{J}x^{K} = \frac{9}{10} & & {}^{K}x^{J} = 1 \\
{}^{K}x^{L} = \frac{9}{10} & & {}^{L}x^{K} = 1 \\
{}^{J}x^{L} = \frac{11}{10} & & {}^{L}x^{J} = 1 \\
\\
{}^{J}y^{KK} = 90 & & {}^{L}y^{KJ} = 0 \\
{}^{J}y^{KL} = 0 & & {}^{L}y^{JJ} = 100 \\
{}^{J}y^{LL} = 110 & & {}^{K}y^{LL} = 90 \\
{}^{L}y^{KK} = 100 & & {}^{K}y^{JJ} = 100
\end{array}
$$

Note that there is no transshipment carried out in the model; i.e., for $K \neq L$, all ${}^{J}y^{KL} = 0$. The same problem was then recalculated with the additional stipulation that the variables be integer valued. The results in this case were as follows:

$$
\begin{array}{llll}
{}^{J}x^{K} = 1 & & {}^{K}x^{J} = 1 \\
{}^{K}x^{L} = 1 & & {}^{L}x^{K} = 1 \\
{}^{J}x^{L} = 1 & & {}^{L}x^{J} = 1 \\
\\
{}^{J}y^{KK} = 90 & & {}^{L}y^{KJ} = 0 \\
{}^{J}y^{KL} = 10 & & {}^{L}y^{JJ} = 100 \\
{}^{J}y^{LL} = 100 & & {}^{K}y^{LL} = 100 \\
{}^{L}y^{KK} = 100 & & {}^{K}y^{JJ} = 100
\end{array}
$$

The available space on an already assigned aircraft was utilized and transshipment occurred.[21]

[21] An interesting feature of the integer-programming calculation process may have emerged in the problem. In any event, it is worthy of further investigation. By pivoting always in the same row (selected initially because it contained the largest fractional element), it soon became clear that a definite pattern was emerging with regard to the left-hand column elements (the solution values which were to become integers in each successive transformed matrix). These series were as follows:

(*a*) For the pivot row —

1st iteration:

$$\frac{9}{10} + \left(\frac{1}{100}\right)\left(\frac{9}{10}\right)\left(\frac{100}{99}\right) = \frac{9}{10} + \left(\frac{9}{10}\right)\left(\frac{1}{99}\right) = \frac{9}{10}\left(1 + \frac{1}{99}\right) = \frac{10}{11}$$

2nd iteration:

$$\frac{10}{11} + \left(\frac{1}{99}\right)\left(\frac{10}{11}\right)\left(\frac{99}{98}\right) = \frac{10}{11} + \left(\frac{10}{11}\right)\left(\frac{1}{98}\right) = \frac{10}{11}\left(1 + \frac{1}{98}\right) = \frac{990}{1078}$$

This may be generalized:

$$\left(\frac{9}{10}\right)\left(1 + \frac{1}{99}\right)\left(1 + \frac{1}{98}\right)\left(1 + \frac{1}{97}\right)\cdots \quad \text{or} \quad \left(\frac{9}{10}\right)\left(\frac{100}{99}\right)\left(\frac{99}{98}\right)\left(\frac{98}{97}\right)\left(\frac{97}{96}\right)\cdots$$

(*b*) For any other row — (row 4 was chosen as an example) —

1st iteration:

$$\frac{11}{10} - \left(\frac{1}{100}\right)\left(\frac{9}{10}\right)\left(\frac{100}{99}\right)$$

The preceding examples may be generalized:

Result I. In a linear programming minimization problem that is designed to allocate demand for transport services on fixed-capacity equipment, where the cost parameters in the objective function are functions of the distance traveled, inclusion of "transshipment variables" (i.e., the ${}^{J}y^{KL}$'s in the problem on pp. 59 and 60) does not ensure transshipment if the problem is formulated as continuous one.

This can be demonstrated as follows: Assume some ${}^{J}\bar{y}^{KL} > 0$ ($K \neq L$). This implies at least an associated ${}^{J}\bar{x}^{K}$ and ${}^{K}\bar{x}^{L}$ (there may be more than one intermediate node) as components in the total cost function elements ${}^{J}x^{K}$ and ${}^{K}x^{L}$. If shipment were direct, ${}^{J}\bar{y}^{LL}$ ($= {}^{J}\bar{y}^{KL}$, where $K = L$) would have an associated ${}^{J}\bar{x}^{L}$ as part of the ${}^{J}x^{L}$ in the objective function. As a consequence of first, the assumed nature of the cost function and second, the shortest-distance property of a straight line between two points,[22] it follows that ${}^{J}c^{L}\,{}^{J}\bar{x}^{L} \leq {}^{J}c^{K}\,{}^{J}\bar{x}^{K} + {}^{K}c^{L}\,{}^{K}\bar{x}^{L}$. Strict inequality would hold whenever the intermediate node K did not lie on a straight line connecting J and L; the equality would perhaps hold when the sum of distances J to K and K to L was equal to the distance from J to L.[23] There is nothing in any of the constraints which dictates that in any ${}^{J}y^{KL}$ term, K should be different from L. Cost minimization thus would favor direct shipment.

2nd iteration:

$$\frac{11}{10} - \left(\frac{1}{100}\right)\left(\frac{9}{10}\right)\left(\frac{100}{99}\right) - \left(\frac{1}{99}\right)\left(\frac{9}{10}\right)\left(\frac{100}{99}\right)\left(\frac{99}{98}\right)$$

In general:

$$\frac{11}{10} - \left(\frac{9}{10}\right)\left(\frac{100}{1}\right)\left[\frac{1}{(99)(100)} + \frac{1}{(98)(99)} + \frac{1}{(97)(98)} + \cdots\right]$$

In *a*, after precisely 10 iterations, the original $\frac{9}{10}$ becomes $\frac{10}{10} = 1$. In *b*, after 10 iterations, the original $\frac{11}{10}$ becomes $\frac{10}{10} = 1$. All relevant first-column elements became integers simultaneously after 10 iterations. In the original example, the second column was always the pivot column (by the rule of smallest absolute value of the ratio of first-row to pivot-row elements, and thanks to a liberal number of zeros in the matrix). Other nonpivot-row elements in this column were either $\frac{1}{100}$, $-\frac{1}{100}$, 1, or -1. The *change* after 10 iterations is thus either $\frac{1}{10}$, $-\frac{1}{10}$, 10, or -10, respectively. The precise relationship between the fractional parts of the optimal noninteger answers (here all tenths or multiples thereof) and the number of iterations necessary and also the importance of zeros and their placement in the matrix deserve additional study.

[22] On a sphere (the globe) the shortest distances are, of course, great-circle routes. The principle still applies, however.

[23] In reality, of course, a one-stop run over the same course as a nonstop run would be more costly because of reductions in over-all speed due to landing and subsequent take-off and attendant landing expenses.

Result II. A requirement that the solution variables of the preceding problem be integers (i.e., formulating it as a discrete problem) assures the consideration of transshipment possibilities in the final solution.

Imagine first the solution values ${}^{J}x^{K}$ of the *continuous* problem. This is the initial step in achieving an integer solution. Some or all of these will have fractional parts, f_{JK}.[24] If the formulation did not contain the y variables, then imposing an integer requirement would result in *increasing* all noninteger solution values to the next highest integer. The inclusion of the y's, however, allows the following sort of comparison to be made. Denote the maximum fractional part of an assignment in an indirect closed path (o) from J to K by $f_{JoK}^{\max}$.[25] If for some direct route J to K, f_{JK} is small enough so that $(1 - f_{JoK}^{\max}) \geq f_{JK}$, then the integer program will make assignments along route o and eliminate one ${}^{J}x^{K}$. This holds for models with one aircraft type, but it can be generalized to multiple equipment systems. In the general case there will be many different points J and K for which such f_{JK}'s exist. Each will have an associated set of f_{JoK}'s, and the numerous various possible alternative routings of marginal passengers must be examined simultaneously. It is sufficient to have shown, however, that transshipment *may* occur from one direct route, J to K, to its associated closed-loop path. Thus it is clear that for at least some types of linear programming problems the actual transshipment character of the model is intimately connected with an integer requirement on the variables. In particular, to have transshipment, one must restrict the results to integers.

It must be pointed out that such an integer program is a theoretic reality only. As yet, the procedure for computing programs with only integer results is not completely satisfactory, although it works without difficulty in many cases. Therefore, although the integer formulation is inherently superior, as it relates to transshipment, the models actually employed in this analysis will be continuous. Results will be rounded to the next highest integer. The value of the objective function will also be increased correspondingly. A case can be made for rounding all figures in this way on the basis of the condition of data

[24] If none contains fractional parts, then the integer requirement, which takes effect only when the (noninteger) optimum to the continuous formulation has been obtained, was never introduced. This unlikely case, therefore, is not properly considered under Result II.

[25] These are not actual routes utilized by passengers from J to K, since all ${}^{J}y^{KL}$ $(K \neq L)$ are zero for the continuous model.

in general in almost any applied study. Conversely, to employ integer-programming methods imparts to the fractional parts of the results more importance then they deserve or than can be justified by inherently imprecise data.

Example 3

Another small example is presented here. Two aircraft types are included in a continuous model, and the data have been selected so that not all routes are more economically served by the same aircraft. The information is the same as that for Example 2, with the addition of the following data, which apply to a second airplane type:

$$
\begin{aligned}
{}^{J}c^{K} &= {}^{K}c^{J} = 30\\
{}^{K}c^{L} &= {}^{L}c^{K} = 40\\
{}^{J}c^{L} &= {}^{L}c^{J} = 80
\end{aligned}
$$

After seven iterations, the following flight assignment results were obtained:

$$
\begin{aligned}
{}^{J}x_1^{K} &= \tfrac{9}{10} \qquad & {}^{K}x_2^{L} &= \tfrac{3}{2}\\
{}^{J}x_1^{L} &= \tfrac{11}{10} \qquad & {}^{L}x_2^{K} &= \tfrac{3}{2}\\
{}^{K}x_1^{J} &= 1 & &\\
{}^{L}x_1^{K} &= \tfrac{1}{10} & &
\end{aligned}
$$

Airplane type 2 (the x_2 values) was inherently more economical on the route between K and L, and it was utilized on that segment. Total cost, \$392, was \$6 lower than in this same model with only one type of airplane available.[26]

Additional nodes could be added to these small noninteger examples without any basic disturbance to former results. That is, in a continuous formulation the geographic relationship of individual nodes to one another does not play a decisive role. Each route is examined as a separate entity, and the most economical aircraft is assigned for the demand on that route.[27] The advantages of passenger consolidation and transshipment are not explored.

This is relevant to a basic point which should be mentioned here.[28] It might be that an analysis of some segment of the domestic trunkline

[26] Compare these assignments with the results of Example 2, which appear on p. 67.

[27] Addition of more and more routes eventually will result in exhaustion of the supply of one or more aircraft types. When that occurs, then the last routes added will have introduced a basic change in the final optimal results.

[28] I am indebted to Professor Jesse Markham, who first brought this to my attention.

industry for a particular year in the past, using a model of the sort developed in this study, indicates large amounts of overscheduling and consequent inefficiency. Perhaps the fault lies entirely within the model, however, and the inclusion of one additional node would produce a result indicating that the system was efficient. This is not difficult to imagine. Apparent overscheduling of flights into New York, for example, might be due to large amounts of traffic continuing on to Philadelphia. If Philadelphia were not included in the model, then this fact would be obscured, and the system would appear to be inefficient.

The important point to be noted, however, is that this applies only to a discrete model in which transshipment is allowed. The continuous formulation defines an inflexible system of direct transportation only. The data employed are therefore direct origin-to-destination figures. In these terms, the question of whether or not the New York–Miami route is described as overscheduled will be decided independently of whether or not Tampa and Atlanta, for example, are in the model. This is not an ideal situation, but it is a consequence of the impossibility of formulating a large, workable integer program.

5. Summary

In this chapter, the rationale for the mathematics used has been explained, and a basic model has been presented. Steps leading to a "master model" have been suggested in Appendix B. If all of these were incorporated, this model would

1. Distinguish the class of all airplane flights, i.e., first-class, coach, or combined configuration.
2. Allow for entry and exit of aircraft from outside the system whose functions would be to alleviate temporary and unanticipated equipment shortages.
3. Explicitly incorporate the problem of optimal routing to maintenance facilities at the proper times for each individual aircraft in the system, recognizing the costs of waiting, should queues be formed.
4. Require integer results.

The first two refinements have not been used in the final model of this study because they necessitated a much more complex formulation that was too large for practical computations at the time they were planned. The third was shown to be less relevant in a system composed of many individual airlines, each of which takes care of its own maintenance problems. The integer requirement is ignored only because of the current state of development of integer-programming computational techniques for large-scale computers. It is to be hoped that this will be overcome in the near future and that analyses such as this one can soon be treated as integer programs. In the next chapter, attention will turn to even more alterations and definitional refinements that are necessary to achieve a workable model.

Chapter 5

The Model: Specific Interpretation

THE GENERAL MODEL presented in the preceding chapter is made more specific in Section 1 of this chapter. Special techniques used in the prediction of parameters for the 1963 model are discussed in Section 2. Section 3 contains some notes on computation and remarks on the problem of accuracy in economic models. Section 4 serves as a summary. Appendix C is concerned with methods of demand forecasting in the air travel market. Appendix D lists all data and sources.

1. Special Problems and Precise Interpretations

A number of problems arise when one prepares to gather data for the model. Most of these require decisions that clarify the exact meanings of terms employed in the formulation. While they do not alter the basic philosophy or function of the model, they should be discussed together at length in order to sharpen its precise meaning. A few general topics will be disposed of initially, and then the model will be examined, term by term, for items that require further clarification.

Unfilled Demand

The unfilled demand terms ${}^{J}d^{L}$ appear in the objective function and in Constraints 1 of the model described on pages 59 and 60. It is entirely proper to assume that an individual airline will consider lost revenue as a cost which should be avoided or at least minimized, and the increased costs associated with additional flights will be weighed against revenue lost to competition and perhaps also public confidence or company reputation. It will be assumed here, however, that a regulatory agency such as the CAB, being vested with the public interest, will interpret that interest as including the efficient movement of *all* persons who wish such service. Thus, their problem will be posed as that of moving all demand at least cost. Therefore, the term $\sum_{J}\sum_{K} {}^{J}p^{K}\,{}^{J}d^{K}$ is removed from the objective function, and ${}^{J}d^{L}$ is taken from the left-hand side of Constraints 1.[1]

Historical and Projective Settings

It is of interest to select a recent year in the past, before the advent of pure-jet air transportation, to examine discrepancies between the solution which the programming analysis gives and the actual scheduling at that time. The last year for which complete data are available in a satisfactory form is 1957, and is the year that has been selected. For projection to a year when pure jets and jet props will be in use almost exclusively, any year after 1961 would be satisfactory. The year 1963 was selected as the frame of reference for this part of the analysis.

Length of Time Period

Even though the above decisions provide settings for the analysis, still another time problem remains. The entire model is constructed to span a given time period; demands, aircraft availabilities, and flight assignments must relate to a time unit basis. Thus the question of the length of this unit becomes relevant. Is the analysis interested in scheduled flights and passenger movements per day, week, month, year, or some other period? The manner in which data are available provides some clue to possible answers. Historical demand data (numbers of passengers transported between any two given points) are in terms of a two-week sample period, tabulated twice a year. This would seem to justify using either a monthly or bimonthly period (perhaps even weekly).

In the model itself do particular constraints imply anything about

[1] Items d also are removed from Constraints 5, of course. One might conclude that the removal of these "lost revenue" terms from the objective function would suggest an obvious way to minimize that function — simply set all x's equal to zero. Constraints 1, in conjunction with 4, are sufficient to prevent such an allocation. At least some nonzero y's are necessary to satisfy the (nonzero) ${}^{J}D^{L}$ in Constraints 1, and through Constraints 4 this implies nonzero levels of at least some (corresponding) x's.

the period? Constraints 1 immediately cause problems. They involve figures, the *D*'s, that denote total demands in the period. But the distribution of these demands throughout the period is not specified. For example, given a demand figure (in the two-week sample period) of 400, the assignment of four flights of aircraft with capacity of 100 each during the two-week period could distort the problem greatly. The demand might have been distributed approximately equally over ten days, indicating the need for (at least) five flights carrying 40 passengers each.

There is the further problem of the distribution of demand within any given day. This introduces a consideration of the characteristics of airline demand, with particular emphasis on the following sort of question: Does an airline tailor its flight schedules to the particular time of day when it thinks passengers wish to be transported, or do potential customers generally adapt their demands to the published times of departure?

From the point of view of the airlines, passenger desires are only one of many considerations, although they are a very important one. Departure times from any given point must be conditioned by first, space and facilities available at consequent arrival times at other important nodes, and second, connections available with other equipment in the same airline and, even more complexly, in other airlines. Not only convenience but also such items as available airport facilities and weather conditions at different times of day are important.[2]

What is the point of view of the passenger? Airline demand is essentially of two sorts: personal and business.[3] Emergency traffic

[2] See "United Air Lines, Scheduling Flight 612," in George P. Baker and Gayton E. Germane, *Case Problems in Transportation Management* (New York: McGraw-Hill Book Company, 1957), pp. 108–114. The question was whether a scheduled 7:30 A.M. departure from Seattle should operate later in the day during months of questionable early morning weather in the Pacific Northwest. It is of interest that demand considerations were based mainly on revenue which could be captured by competitors' flights and on reputation of dependability through nondelay of scheduled departures, except that there did seem to be recognition of an early morning "boundary" before which passengers could not be expected to appear at the airport: "Flight 612's departure time from Seattle had been set at 0730, since prior to 0700 was considered too early to attract a satisfactory passenger load and since any departure time between 0700 and 0725 would reach Chicago at a period when station ramp facilities were unable to handle additional aircraft," *ibid.*, p. 112.

[3] An interesting discussion of these two segments of the air travel market is provided in Exhibit AA-11, "Testimony of Walter H. Johnson, Jr.," American Airlines, Vol. VIII, pp. 4–9, in *General Passenger Fare Investigation*. Personal travel is further subdivided into that undertaken for family reasons because of population shifts (largely motivated by "emotional considerations") and vacation trips.

is a small proportion of total traffic and is almost always on the "soonest possible flight" basis. Approximate division of total airline travel has been estimated by a number of writers. These are indicated in Table 5-1. Insofar as this table was prepared only to indicate the general relationship between business and pleasure travel, it is not necessary to dwell upon details and discrepancies. It will be mentioned in passing only that the introduction and rapid public acceptance of coach accommodations may account in a large part for the increased use of air travel for personal reasons.[4]

TABLE 5-1. AIRLINE DEMAND

Year	Business Reasons	Personal Reasons	Combined Reasons
	Per Cent of Total Actual or Forecast Trips taken for		
1948	78.8	21.2[a]	
1950	59.6	40.4[b]	
1955	52.9	47.1[b]	
1955	55.0	45.0[c]	
1955	36.0	64.0[d]	
1955–1956 (winter)	41.0	48.0	11.0[e]
1956 (summer)	45.0	45.0	10.0[f]
1957	48.0	52.0[g]	
1965	56.9	43.1[h]	
1975	61.2	38.8[h]	
1980	53.3	46.7[i]	

Sources:

a. (Actual traffic for New York — Northeastern New Jersey sample area) Port of New York Authority, *Air Traffic Forecasts, 1950–1980* (New York: Port of New York Authority, Department of Airport Development, 1950), p. 27.

b. (Estimates) Port of New York Authority, Aviation Department, *Air Travel Forecasting, 1965–1975* (New York: Columbia University Press, 1957), p. 56.

c. Cherington, *op. cit.*, p. 35.

d. University of Michigan Survey of Reasons for Air Travel, cited in Jesse J. Friedman, "Comparative Study of the Investment-Profit Structure of the Airline Industry, Testimony on behalf of the Air Transport Association of America" (Washington: Jesse J. Friedman and Associates, 1957), p. 32.

e. Port of New York Authority, *Survey of Reasons for Air Travel* (Winter, 1955–1956), cited in Friedman, *loc. cit.*

f. Port of New York Authority, *Survey of Reasons for Air Travel* (Summer, 1956), cited in *ibid.*

g. U.S. Department of Commerce estimates, quoted in "Testimony of Walter H. Johnson, Jr.," *op. cit.*, Appendix B.

h. Same as note b, at p. 54.

i. Same as note a, at p. 27.

To the passenger who travels for personal reasons, the time of day at which a flight departs is perhaps not of crucial importance. Assume that *all* airlines decided to operate all flights between any two given

[4] See Paul W. Cherington, *Airline Price Policy: A Study of Domestic Airline Passenger Fares* (Boston: Harvard University, Graduate School of Business Administration, 1958), p. 37; also "Testimony of Walter H. Johnson, Jr.," *loc. cit.*

points at a single point of time (or within narrow bounds) each day. What would be the probable reaction of persons traveling for these non-business reasons? Undoubtedly, plans would adapt almost completely to such a change. At most, they might be shifted by one day in either direction.

Persons demanding air travel accommodations for business reasons, however, might place somewhat more emphasis on the particular time of departure within any day. Therefore, a concentration of flights at a specific hour might cause a shift of some traffic to other modes of transportation. The longer the distance to be covered, the less likely this shift would be.[5]

Thus it will be suggested that it is legitimate to represent daily demand between any two nodes as concentrated at a single point of time within that day. This same argument cannot be extended to longer time periods, e.g., to justify the concentration of weekly demand at a single point of time within the week. Constraints 2, 3, and 4, and the objective function itself retain their general validity regardless of the time period chosen. Constraints 1 argue for a daily period, and the demand figures, as they are available, adapt themselves best to monthly, bimonthly or weekly analysis.

This study will compromise the two positions and deal with weekly demands, and consequently with weekly flight schedules. It may be an unhappy choice, but all other alternatives seem to have equally strong or stronger drawbacks. The assumptions that this procedure implies regarding airline demand are fully recognized and discussed in the next chapter as contributing to the differences that are observed when comparing actual and theoretical results.[6]

[5] Optimistic observers would even question this. See, for example, "Testimony of Walter H. Johnson, Jr.," *ibid.*, pp. 4–6.

[6] Moreover, the other most logical possibility, treating demand on a daily basis, also involved difficulties. Suppose, as a first approximation, that demand is assumed to be divided equally among the seven days in the week. Then the problem of too few assignments (see p. 75) can be avoided by treating Constraints 1 on a daily basis, i.e., dividing weekly demand by seven, and by entering the multiplier seven as a coefficient wherever a y-term appears. Perhaps even more realistic would be an assumption of demand distributed equally over five days in the week, thus leaving room for the not unusual phenomenon of flights that are not scheduled for every day of the week. Even though this would not require that the particular five days be specified, it would lead to the unsatisfactory result that all nodes in the system would be inactive on the same two days. Finally, to allow for an uneven distribution of demands during the days of the week, while more realistic, would necessitate a much more detailed objective function and set of constraints (recording which day each particular flight was scheduled). Furthermore, it would involve a partially unjustified manipulation of the original passenger traffic data which are not on a differentiated daily basis.

It is now appropriate to specify particular items within the model more clearly[7]

Costs (${}^{J}_{r}c^{K}_{h}$)

These are direct aircraft operating expenses per airplane-mile for aircraft type h (for the length of hop involved) multiplied by mileage between J and K.[8] They incorporate long-haul economies. No distinction will be made for various capacities; the r subscript can be dropped.

Demands (${}^{J}D^{K}$)

Actual historical data on airline passenger movement between any two domestic nodes are quite good. The figures are based on a two-week sample period and are compiled twice each year, during March and September. Unfortunately, these are not really demand figures, for there is no real way of knowing how many people desired service but were not accommodated. Such information is seldom recorded by an airline. Herein lies another justification for dropping untransported demand from the model.

There would seem to be two solutions regarding classes of traffic: Either one can assume that all movement is first-class traffic, with appropriate aircraft capacities, or else one can devise a "composite configuration" of part first class and part coach.[9] The former is more appropriate for 1957, when coach travel was not as important as it has now become. It will be used in the historical model. The latter is more realistic for the future, because most of the large jets will operate with a combined configuration; it will be used in the projective model. Furthermore, most forecasts are on a total passenger demand basis; to try to break these into coach and first-class figures would involve further assumptions.

[7] All data for both 1957 and 1963 are listed in Appendix D along with sources.

[8] Expenses per airplane-mile are almost universally accepted in industry use, whereas expenses per flight-hour are not. While mileage between two nodes may vary because of deviations from a straight-line course, the elapsed flying time is subject to more error, and thus costs between the nodes based on per-flight-hour expenses are much more variable.

[9] Note that the ticket price, which would be different depending on which of these methods was employed, is no longer of any relevance because untransported demand does not enter into the operational model.

The Availability Constraints and a Measure of Stock (S_h)

Before dealing with the problem of converting aircraft availability into hours, it is necessary to establish how the numbers of planes themselves will be known. An example illustrates the problem: Assume that New York–Los Angeles and also New York–Boston are among those routes considered. Assume further that New York–Los Angeles is served by United Air Lines, Trans World Airlines, and American Airlines and the Boston run by Eastern Air Lines and Northeast Airlines. To consider the equipment of all five airlines as available in the model would be to run the risk that the programming analysis will suggest switching some aircraft between these two runs. This is clearly difficult if not impossible under the existing market structure, but from the point of view of an efficiency analysis, it is precisely the sort of problem that one is likely to discover.[10]

Once the given number of aircraft of a particular type has been established, a downward adjustment of this figure is necessary to allow for equipment undergoing overhaul and allocated as "spare." Information supplied chiefly by the airlines themselves suggests approximately 3 per cent and 6 per cent, respectively, as appropriate reductions of each aircraft type to allow for these factors.[11]

With the previous adjustments in numbers of aircraft, the problem of converting these figures to available hours still remains. This is accomplished by multiplying average number of hours utilization per day (for a particular aircraft type) by seven, the number of days in the time period; this figure is then multiplied by the number of aircraft. Hours of utilization for major domestic trunks were averaged, to arrive

[10] It is for reasons of exactly this sort that the CAB is asked to take a more comprehensive view when deciding new route cases and consequent flight scheduling. At first glance, one might be inclined to argue that there should be no availability constraint at all; the CAB should have power even to direct equipment purchases (or, less directly, to specify equipment to be used on routes awarded) after having made an efficiency analysis with various available equipment types but no constraints. The Board must work within some (perhaps wide) limits, however, and for available aircraft in this model these limits will be taken to be all domestic trunkline equipment, thereby transcending particular airlines. It is readily admitted that such an interpretation allows the possibility of removing aircraft from other trunkline routes which are not included in the model, but insofar as the routes to be analyzed are the ones of most importance to the public (i.e., the most heavily traveled ones), such a conclusion is perhaps defensible.

[11] Letters to the writer from officials of Delta Air Lines, Trans World Airlines, and Northwest Airlines. See overhaul figures in *American Aviation,* December 15, 1958, p. 25.

at a figure for daily hours of utilization of each aircraft type. The number of available hours for the entire time period for each equipment results.[12]

In both models it has been necessary to aggregate to four basic aircraft types. For the 1957 model, the DC-7C, DC-6B, Viscount 700, and CV-340 are the representative aircraft of the categories 1, 2, 3, and 4, respectively. In the 1963 model, the 707, 720, Electra, and Viscount are used. The equipment operating data and characteristics are for these representative aircraft, but availability figures include other airplane types that have been distributed among these classifications. Appendix D indicates the aircraft included in each category.

Load Factors (*Subscripts r*)

Clearly the passenger load factor on any given flight can take on any value from zero to 100 per cent of capacity. Indeed, one might think that numerous possible r's should be allowed on each aircraft between any two given points; i.e., for any ${}^{J}_{r}x^{K}_{h}$, the r should take on many values. As the model is set up, however, it is not possible to allow choice among various load factors. Thus several computational runs were made with differing assumed load factors.

From a relatively ideal point of view, it is of interest to assume almost full-capacity flights and examine the scheduling that results. A load factor of 95 per cent was used for this purpose. This would provide the *most* efficient result. However, it will also be of interest to examine possibilities for better allocation, given a figure that was closer to the historical utilization for the year in question. The figure 60 per cent was selected.

Aircraft Time between J and K (${}^{J}b^{K}$)

The figure used is for nonstop flights between points J and K. Since some of the nodes are not currently connected by nonstop

[12] The possibility for improper aggregation, although present, is not particularly dangerous. That is, if three aircraft (assuming 8 hours a day utilization) were assigned to fly 6-hour trips, each would have an available 2 hours which, aggregated, would be an extra 6 hours. In the model there apparently would be time for one more flight. But such flexibility is not undesirable, since the utilization figures are average ones only, and, given the opportunity, no airline objects to more hours of utilization per day. To allow only 8 hours or less on each airplane would be an unrealistic restriction on the equipment. Note that this is an entirely different situation from the improper aggregation of time remaining prior to maintenance, when a prespecified number of hours sets an absolute limit such that remaining 3 hours on two aircraft cannot combine to accommodate a 6-hour flight.

flights, data will be derived from division of published air-miles by average block speed for each aircraft type. The speed figure includes take-off and landing time and taxiing. Average attainable block speeds vary for length of haul in such a way that longer hauls permit higher average speeds. Thus, different speeds will be used, depending on the classification into which the mileage between J and K falls.

Final Formulation and the Dual

It is now appropriate to summarize and examine the final resulting framework. The ${}^Jd^L$ terms may be removed. For the continuous formulation in which no transshipment occurs, K equals L for all ${}^Jy^{KL}$. Thus Constraints 1, $\sum_K {}^Jy^{KL} - \sum {}^Ky^{JL} = {}^JD^L$, become simply ${}^Jy^{KK} = {}^JD^K$ for all J and K, where K is now used to designate final destination. This can be substituted into Constraints 4:

$$\sum_h \sum_r {}^J_ra^K_h \, {}^J_rx^K_h - {}^Jy^{KK} \geq 0$$

or

$$\sum_h \sum_r {}^J_ra^K_h \, {}^J_rx^K_h - {}^JD^K \geq 0$$

finally

$$\sum_h \sum_r {}^J_ra^K_h \, {}^J_rx^K_h \geq {}^JD^K$$

Constraints 1 are thereby eliminated, reducing the size of the problem.

In final form, the primal problem here discussed would be as follows:

Minimize: $$\sum_J \sum_K \sum_h {}^Jc^K_h \, {}^Jx^K_h$$

Subject to:

$$1. \quad \sum_K {}^Kx^J_h - \sum_K {}^Jx^K_h \geq 0$$

$$2. \quad -\sum_J \sum_K {}^Jb^K_h \, {}^Jx^K_h \geq -S_h$$

$$3. \quad \sum_h {}^Ja^K_h \, {}^Jx^K_h \geq {}^JD^K$$

In all constraints,

$$J = 1, \cdots, U; \quad K = 1, \cdots, (U - 1); \quad h = 1, \cdots, t; \quad J \neq K$$

A small example, with one aircraft type, one capacity, and three nodes (New York, Chicago, and Los Angeles) would be

Minimize:

$$ {}^{N}c^{C}\,{}^{N}x^{C}+{}^{C}c^{L}\,{}^{C}x^{L}+{}^{N}c^{L}\,{}^{N}x^{L}+{}^{C}c^{N}\,{}^{C}x^{N}+{}^{L}c^{C}\,{}^{L}x^{C}+{}^{L}c^{N}\,{}^{L}x^{N} $$

Subject to:

$$
\begin{array}{lllllllll}
1. & +{}^{N}x^{C} & -{}^{C}x^{L} & & -{}^{C}x^{N} & +{}^{L}x^{C} & & \geq & 0 \\
 & & +{}^{C}x^{L} & +{}^{N}x^{L} & & -{}^{L}x^{C} & -{}^{L}x^{N} & \geq & 0 \\
 & -{}^{N}x^{C} & & -{}^{N}x^{L} & +{}^{C}x^{N} & & +{}^{L}x^{N} & \geq & 0 \\
2. & -{}^{N}b^{C}\,{}^{N}x^{C} & -{}^{C}b^{L}\,{}^{C}x^{L} & -{}^{N}b^{L}\,{}^{N}x^{L} & -{}^{C}b^{N}\,{}^{C}x^{N} & -{}^{L}b^{C}\,{}^{L}x^{C} & -{}^{L}b^{N}\,{}^{L}x^{N} & \geq & -S \\
 & {}^{N}a^{C}\,{}^{N}x^{C} & & & & & & \geq & {}^{N}D^{C} \\
3. & & {}^{C}a^{L}\,{}^{C}x^{L} & & & & & \geq & {}^{C}D^{L} \\
 & & & {}^{N}a^{L}\,{}^{N}x^{L} & & & & \geq & {}^{N}D^{L} \\
 & & & & {}^{C}a^{N}\,{}^{C}x^{N} & & & \geq & {}^{C}D^{N} \\
 & & & & & {}^{L}a^{C}\,{}^{L}x^{C} & & \geq & {}^{L}D^{C} \\
 & & & & & & {}^{L}a^{N}\,{}^{L}x^{N} & \geq & {}^{L}D^{N}
\end{array}
$$

For the same three-node example, the dual would be as follows:[13]

Maximize:

$$ 0\,{}^{C}v+0\,{}^{N}v+0\,{}^{L}v-Sw+{}^{N}D^{C}\,{}^{N}u^{C}+{}^{C}D^{L}\,{}^{C}u^{L}+{}^{N}D^{L}\,{}^{N}u^{L}+{}^{C}D^{N}\,{}^{C}u^{N}+{}^{L}D^{C}\,{}^{L}u^{C}+{}^{L}D^{N}\,{}^{L}u^{N} $$

Subject to:

$$
\begin{array}{llllllllllll}
+{}^{C}v & -{}^{N}v & & -{}^{N}b^{C}\,w & +{}^{N}a^{C}\,{}^{N}u^{C} & & & & & & \leq & {}^{N}c^{C} \\
-{}^{C}v & & +{}^{L}v & -{}^{C}b^{L}\,w & & +{}^{C}a^{L}\,{}^{C}u^{L} & & & & & \leq & {}^{C}c^{L} \\
 & -{}^{N}v & +{}^{L}v & -{}^{N}b^{L}\,w & & & +{}^{N}a^{L}\,{}^{N}u^{L} & & & & \leq & {}^{N}c^{L} \\
-{}^{C}v & +{}^{N}v & & -{}^{C}b^{N}\,w & & & & +{}^{C}a^{N}\,{}^{C}u^{N} & & & \leq & {}^{C}c^{N} \\
+{}^{C}v & & -{}^{L}v & -{}^{L}b^{C}\,w & & & & & +{}^{L}a^{C}\,{}^{L}u^{C} & & \leq & {}^{L}c^{C} \\
 & +{}^{N}v & -{}^{L}v & -{}^{L}b^{N}\,w & & & & & & +{}^{L}a^{N}\,{}^{L}u^{N} & \leq & {}^{L}c^{N}
\end{array}
$$

The relationships between primal and dual problems have, among others, the following properties: For a variable whose value is positive in the optimal solution to one problem, the corresponding constraint in the associated problem is met with exact equality. From this it can be seen that a constraint met with strict inequality in one problem implies that the optimal solution value of the corresponding variable in the associated problem will be zero.[14]

The following interpretations may be placed on the variables in the dual.[15] The quantity ${}^{J}v_{h}$ is an imputed rent (a storage cost, in a sense) on a unit of aircraft type h at node J. Basically this is a hypothetical cost that an airline should be willing to pay in order to have a single airplane of type h available at J. When the stock of spares at

[13] See any of the standard linear programming references, e.g., those in footnote 1, p. 54, for a discussion of the relationship between the primal and the dual problems.

[14] Cf. R. Dorfman, P. A. Samuelson, and R. Solow, *Linear Programming and Economic Analysis* (New York ; McGraw-Hill Book Company, Inc., 1958), p. 44. Note that it is *not* always true either that exact equality in a constraint implies a corresponding variable which is positive valued, or that a zero-valued variable always implies an inequality constraint.

[15] From this point on it is easier to think of these balance constraints in their more general form, i.e., with a term $-\sigma$ on the right-hand side of the inequality. Thus, for node j, $+{}^{J}\sigma_{h}$ represents the stock of type h aircraft on hand during the period, and it enters with a negative sign in order to preserve the consistent direction for minimization problems.

any particular node is not exhausted, i.e., when extra spares remain at a point, the primal-dual relationship just stated suggests that the firms concerned would be unwilling to pay any positive amount for their availability; the appropriate v would be zero. This is consistent with the way in which these variables enter into the constraints of the dual. Movement from J to K subtracts an amount ${}^{J}v$ and adds an amount ${}^{K}v$ to the imputed net profit because the likelihood of exhausting the stock at J has been increased while the stock at K has been augmented.

Item w_h may be thought of as the imputed value (interpreted as a charge, i.e., as a toll in a highway problem) of an hour's travel over any air route on aircraft type h. Finally, the ${}^{J}u^{K}$ are values of a delivered unit of commodity (passenger) over the route J to K. Thus the constraints in the dual require that the cost of movement of a transport vehicle over the route from J to K be no less than the imputed net profit for the movement. They express zero profit conditions; for those primal activities that are actually undertaken (${}^{J}x_h^K > 0$), profits will be zero (dual constraints will be met with equality); a dual constraint that is a strict inequality (profits less than costs) will have an associated ${}^{J}x_h^K = 0$. Maximization of the objective function amounts to the maximization of total imputed net profit.

In general terms, then, the dual of the formulation used in this study is

$$\text{Maximize:} \quad -\sum_J \sum_h {}^{J}\sigma_h \, {}^{J}v_h - \sum_h S_h \, w_h + \sum_J \sum_K {}^{J}D^{K} \, {}^{J}u^{K}$$

Subject to:

$$-{}^{J}v_h + {}^{K}v_h - {}^{J}b_h^K \, w_h + {}^{J}a_h^K \, {}^{J}u^K \leq {}^{J}c_h^K \quad \text{(for each } h\text{)},$$

$$\text{and} \quad u, v, w, \geq 0,$$

where

$$J = 1, \cdots, U; \quad K = 1, \cdots, (U-1); \quad J \neq K; \quad h = 1, \cdots, t$$

For a form of more interest to a particular airline, the inclusion of untransported demand can be accomplished through the addition of a set of terms $-{}^{J}p^{K}\,{}^{J}d^{K}$ in the objective function of the primal and a diagonal set of $-{}^{J}d^{L}$ terms to Constraints 4 in the primal. The dual would then have an additional set of constraints: $-{}^{J}u^{K} \leq -{}^{J}p^{L}$.

Scope of the Problems

For both 1957 and 1963 studies, an intercity and an interregional model were formed. The intercity model contains nine cities that have consistently been among the top twelve in terms of total passenger traffic over a period of many years. The cities are New York, Chicago, Miami, Los Angeles, Washington, San Francisco, Detroit, Boston, and Cleveland. The interregional model attempts to achieve a more thorough geographical coverage of the United States, and it is able to do so largely through ignoring traffic flows within individual regions. Seven geographical sectors are used; the cities involved in each are (1) New York, Washington, Boston, Philadelphia; (2) Chicago, Detroit, St. Louis, Cleveland; (3) Miami; (4) Los Angeles, San Francisco; (5) Seattle; (6) Dallas; (7) Atlanta. These represent the most significant air traffic generating areas.

Thus there are two models, the intercity and the interregional, for each of two years, 1957 and 1963, and each is solved for two different assumed load factors, 60 per cent and 95 per cent.

2. Data Sources and Projections

It is of specific interest in this study to consider a future set of demands as well as data from the recent past. In the latter case, of course, the historical record already exists, and thus it becomes possible to compare theoretical with actual results. In the former case, interest is attached to the usefulness in planning operations to meet possible future demands upon the system. Appendix D contains complete data listings and sources for each of the particular programs solved in this study. It will be necessary here to discuss only the techniques employed in deriving some of the figures for the 1963 projection model.

The area of demand projection and analysis, both in general and for the domestic airline industry in particular, is worthy of a complete study in itself. Extensive investigation or documentation of this area has not been possible within the confines of this study. Appendix C has been included for the purpose of describing briefly several existing types of projection studies that have been applied to air travel. The following subsections include a discussion of the methods employed here.

Demand Figures

The following technique was used to arrive at a forecast for demands on each individual route in 1963:

1. The Civil Aeronautics Administration forecast of 82.2 million passengers on domestic airlines for 1963 forms a basis for all

calculations.[16] As is seen in Appendix C, many airlines and other private organizations prepare their own forecasts. These, however, are usually in terms of total passenger-miles, not passengers, and they tend to be widely divergent. The CAA shows a good record in past projections.

2. The total of 82.2 million passengers was multiplied by a route percentage for each individual route — a figure that estimates the percentage of total domestic passengers expected to move along each given air route. To derive this percentage estimate, observations were made of recorded traffic over each route considered during the period 1954–1958 inclusive.[17] The figure of weekly passengers traveling over each route was divided by total national passengers recorded for each year to give the per cent of total traffic that moved along each route in each of the five years. With time measured along the horizontal axis and route per cent of national traffic on the vertical axis, a scatter of five points was thus derived for each route. A least-squares regression line was fitted and projected to 1963. This provided a percentage figure for probable traffic on each given route. These are the route percentage estimates that were multiplied by 82.2 million to give the absolute number of passengers.

Several general comments can be made regarding this procedure:

a. There is extensive evidence to support the assertion that a city's percentage share of the total United States' passenger market is relatively constant.[18] This is an important finding. Given such a hypothesis of constant total percentages for the cities in question, the projections developed in this study may be thought of as estimates of

[16] See U.S., Civil Aeronautics Administration, *Operating the Jet* (Washington, D. C.; U.S. Government Printing Office, 1958), p. 82; also U.S., Congress, House, Subcommittee of the Committee on Government Operations, Hearings, *Federal Role In Aviation*, 84th Cong., 2nd Sess., 1956, p. 1080.

[17] Data for each year are from the two *Origination–Destination Airline Revenue Passenger Surveys*, March and September, for those years.

[18] This is the conclusion of the CAA. It is borne out by reference to the figures presented in their annual *Air Commerce Traffic Pattern.* (Now compiled by the FAA.) Cf., for example, the 1958 issue: "Eleven years of traffic data have demonstrated that a community's percentage share of the United States passenger market is relatively stable," U.S., Civil Aeronautics Administration, *Air Commerce Traffic Pattern* (Washington, D. C.; U.S. Government Printing Office, 1958), p. 3. Cf. also John E. Peterson, *Airports for Jets* (Chicago: American Society of Planning Officials, 1959), for reiteration and support of these findings, esp. pp. 12 ff. This is also an implicit assumption in the forecasts of the Port of New York Authority for the period 1950–1980. See Port of New York Authority, *Air Traffic Forecasts, 1950–1980, op. cit.*, Appendix II, Part I, pp. 363 ff., esp. steps 1, 2, and 3.

the trend in the relative shares of different routes in the total activity of a particular pair of cities. That is, to specify no trend, i.e., to project the mean value of the observations, would involve hypothesizing only that a given route between two cities receives a constant percentage of the total traffic of those cities. In fact, this would involve assuming a constant national percentage, but only because the constancy of a given city's share of the national total has already been hypothesized.

b. It is recognized that projection beyond an observed range by means of any fitted curve, linear or curvilinear, is statistically dangerous. Nonetheless, CAA studies over a period longer than the one here considered indicate certain long-term factors that are relevant to air traffic generation.[19] Important among these are a specific "hub" designation, which is a measure of traffic originations or generating ability, and also the distance between hub sizes.[20]

Particular economic conditions for given years would probably introduce little variation into these figures. For as traffic on a route might decline in a recession, so would total national traffic. There might be different changes between routes which are significant business runs and those which are more important for pleasure travelers. Even here, however, it is difficult to argue the case very far. If New York–Chicago is an important business route and New York–Miami is pleasure oriented, the drop in business travel, though more immediately felt in a general slump, would probably soon be mirrored in a decrease in expensive vacation travel also. Which would be relatively stronger is not easy to say.

It is true that there may be arguments in terms of differential population growth of cities, e.g., the West Coast as compared with the Northeast. For example, an increasingly greater proportion of total New York originations might terminate in Los Angeles. Presumably this fact would show up partly in increasing percentages of total domestic traffic attributable to the growing cities, but this is not

[19] Note, too, that the International Civil Aviation Organization bases estimates of future global demand for air transport on a straightforward projection over future years of the trend observed between 1950 and 1957; namely, an increase of 15 per cent per year in passenger-miles. See International Civil Aviation Organization, *The Economic Implications of the Introduction into Service of Long-Range Jet Aircraft* (Montreal: International Civil Aviation Organization, 1958), p. 19.

[20] "The flow of air transportation is largely controlled by the location of air traffic hubs and the distance between them. . . . The hub designation for a community has a continuity through time. While changes do occur the degree of change is too little to be significant," U.S., Civil Aeronautics Administration, *Air Commerce Traffic Pattern, loc. cit.*

substantiated in the CAA findings of relatively constant percentages of the national total for each large city considered here. Nonetheless, the relative positions of a particular city's individual routes may be shifting in such a way that, for example, there is a positive trend for New York–Los Angeles and a negative one for New York–Cleveland.

c. Instead of accepting the least-squares regression line and projecting five years into the future, it might be tempting to test the hypothesis that the true value of the population correlation coefficient is zero, i.e., to see whether or not the variables are really uncorrelated.[21] But note that on the basis of the argument in *b*, there seems to be no particular justification in assuming that the trend will be either zero or *any* particular value, positive or negative. One should properly test the hypothesis by using some value that is strongly suspected to be the population value. The test might not reject the null hypothesis that, on the basis of the sample, the population correlation coefficient was zero. Another test that $\rho = -0.15$ or even that $\rho = +0.12$ also might not be rejected.[22]

Available Aircraft

Orders for medium- and long-range jets for delivery through 1962 were available in various issues of *Aviation Week* and *American Aviation.* Estimates of domestic trunkline capacity were also provided

[21] The procedure would be to test H_o: $\rho_{21} = 0$ with a *t*-test, where

$$t = \sqrt{[(n-2)r_{21}^2]/(1-r_{21}^2)}$$

and r is the sample correlation coefficient. Note that this test is identical to one for the hypothesis that β_{21}, the population regression coefficient (estimated by b, the slope of the regression line), equals zero. To test H_o: $\beta_{21} = 0$, use

$$t = (s_1\sqrt{n-2}/s_2\sqrt{1-r_{21}^2})\, b_{21}$$

But since $b_{21} = r_{21}\,(s_2/s_1)$, the tests are identical.

[22] Thus, to act on the basis of one hypothesis test and to disregard the slope indicated by a least-squares regression line would seem to be unwise.

The important point is that, for a general method, there is no reason to hypothesize any particular value or values for ρ (or β), and thus testing of hypotheses seems of limited use here.

The justification for the use of least-square methods on time series data can be found in H. Cramer, *The Elements of Probability Theory* (New York: John Wiley & Sons, Inc., 1955), pp. 243–245 (esp. example on p. 245); F. E. Croxton and D. J. Cowden, *Practical Business Statistics* (2nd ed., New York: Prentice-Hall, Inc., 1948), Chapter 13, "Measurement of and Adjustment for Secular Trend," or H. Arkin and R. R. Colton, *Statistical Methods* (4th ed., New York: Barnes & Noble, Inc., 1955), pp. 56–59; and also J. Durbin, "Estimation of Parameters in Time-Series Regression Models," *Journal of the Royal Statistical Society* (Series B — Methodological), XXII (1960), 139–153. The second and third references illustrate extrapolations for a short distance into the future.

by a major airframe manufacturer. The utilization figures for these aircraft were taken from projections made by the airlines. For the most part, these were continuations of 1960 trends of approximately 9 hours per day. Spares allocation and maintenance programs were also assumed to be those in use in 1960 or announced as planned by the major trunks. Capacities and speeds were averages provided by manufacturers, adjusted on the basis of available operating experience.

3. Notes on Accuracy and Computation

Economists have been wisely counseled to examine carefully the data with which they work.[23] This is particularly relevant in view of the tremendous recent increase in quantitative economic analysis. Linear programming is one of the techniques mentioned explicitly.

It is clear that the accuracy of the results of any quantitative analysis depends on several distinct facets of that analysis, any one of which may contribute an amount of error to the result. Among these are

1. The degree to which the model used portrays the reality that it is designed to represent.
2. The accuracy of the data employed in application of the model.
3. The computational errors that may arise during the course of operations. This means, essentially, internal machine rounding errors that can occur in modern computers. It is of interest to comment briefly on each of these points as it pertains to the present analysis.

Regarding 1, it has been the aim of this study to achieve a balance between the more completely descriptive model sketched in Chapter 4 and the more feasible, operational model proposed earlier in the present chapter. For the relatively small number of nodes considered, the final model here employed is felt to be an accurate representation of the air traffic system in operation. Its greatest shortcoming is perhaps in the way demand is assumed to be distributed over the weekly time period. This fact is kept in mind during the analysis of final results.

It is at item 2 that the sharpest comments are frequently leveled. Clearly, the accuracy of the results of any analysis is intimately

[23] Cf. O. Morgenstern, *On the Accuracy of Economic Observations* (Princeton: Princeton University Press, 1950), and Chapter 16 in T. Koopmans (ed.), *Activity Analysis of Production and Allocation* (New York: John Wiley & Sons, Inc., 1951).

affected by the accuracy of the data employed.[24] All known sources have been scrutinized in an effort to obtain the most reliable estimates. Moreover, the formulations used in this study contain many $+1$, -1, and 0 coefficients in the matrix. The models themselves are subject to criticism under point 1, but, once accepted as sufficiently close to reality, there is a greatly decreased number of unknown coefficients in the problem which must be estimated or otherwise provided from observed data.[25]

In particular:

1. Total available stocks, the S's, are based on CAB reports of total trunkline aircraft equipment ownership. This is taken as of December, 1957. Thus it may overstate newly purchased equipment availability and understate older equipment that operated for part of the year before being phased out.

2. Demand data for the routes, the ${}^{J}D^{K}$ items, are composed of complete reporting to the CAB over two separate two-week periods by each domestic trunkline. All figures in this area are averages over airlines and over time.

3. Cost data, the c's, are derived from statistics on Form 41, reported directly to the CAB, either monthly or quarterly by all airlines. The published CAB cost aggregates for each type of aircraft are most frequently available and best used in terms of cost per airplane-mile. They are total mileage logged by each aircraft type within a given time period over specific route lengths divided into total direct aircraft operating expenses chargeable to that equipment type.

The computational errors due to rounding, item 3, which may cause concern when one is working with digital computers, are avoided to as great an extent as is possible in the present example. Calculations for the problems outlined here were made on an IBM 7090 at the Arlington, Virginia, offices of C-E-I-R, Inc. (Corporation for Economic and Industrial Research). The program used, which is a modification of the highly successful SCROL method, contains a

[24] A relatively extensive investigation was made of the probable effects of possible observational errors on the final solution values of the linear programs used in this study. The major result of this investigation was that it seems highly unlikely that great injustice is being done by employing the data as they are available. There is a strong tendency for errors either to cancel out or else progressively to diminish in strength.

[25] The density of a problem may be defined as the ratio of the number of nonzero elements to total number of elements. In the problems that were solved in this study, the density ranged from 0.032 to 0.049; i.e., it was low.

number of internal checks and, through a great deal of use, has become extremely efficient.

Double-precision arithmetic is employed throughout, and this is a highly important feature in large-scale problems for handling round-off error. Such error, if insufficiently controlled, can lead to perturbations of the problem in such a way that erroneous vectors are selected; i.e., incorrect activities are introduced into the basis. This can occur at some point in the calculations through incorrect choice either of a pivot column or of the pivot element in that column, or both. It is further clear that if all elements are subjected to the same relative amount of error (and in the same direction), then the introduction of an improper activity into the basis will probably not occur.[26] Prior to SCROL and machines of the size of the IBM 704 or larger, double-precision arithmetic was extremely costly in terms of machine time, although successful from the point of view of reducing such error.[27]

4. Summary

In studies that include both a theoretical development of some particular technique and an application of the model to a specific problem, the transition from abstract representation to actual reality is usually laborious. It involves unanticipated questions regarding the exact meanings of terms employed and the precise interpretations of available data. Working with the benefit of hindsight, it has been the aim of this chapter to indicate, in two stages, the way in which such a transition has been accomplished in this study. These are first, the formulation of a workable model from the larger, more complex one presented and developed in Chapter 4, and second, the precise interpretation of each term used in the model, with emphasis on the source from which estimates of the particular parameters must come. The problems of demand projections and certain aircraft data for the 1963 model were treated separately in Section 2, and a discussion of machine computations and possible errors was included in Section 3. Preparation is therefore complete, and the results and conclusions of the final chapter may be examined.

[26] Many papers discuss ways of examining effects of errors on the final optimum value of the objective function, assuming always that the round-off error is not large enough to have produced the sort of improper choice mentioned in the text here. Cf., for example, K. W. Webb, "The Mathematical Theory of Sensitivity" (C-E-I-R, Inc., 1960, mimeographed), pp. 15–19.

[27] See W. Jacobs, "Loss of Accuracy in Simplex Computations," *Naval Research Logistics Quarterly, IV* (March, 1957), esp. 94.

Chapter 6

Results and Conclusions

THE RESULTS of the programming problems are presented, and a number of conclusions or inferences are suggested in this, the final chapter. It is necessary to reemphasize the fact that the models used represent only a segment of the domestic air transport industry and that more conclusive evidence would be supported by larger models covering years other than the ones studied here. The rather limited scope of this project was set by a number of external constraints, but in spite of this it is possible to indicate some general hypotheses that seem to be borne out by the results.

The reasons for selection of the particular time periods have been discussed. Results for the 1957 models allow comparisons between observed historical values of particular variables and the solution values of the same variables in an idealized, theoretical formulation such as that used in this study. In particular, it becomes possible to quantify the aircraft scheduling inefficiencies of that year and then to separate the figures into particular routes and to assign a dollar cost to each of them. The 1963 results, on the other hand, illustrate the use of such models as planning devices whereby aggregate demands can be transformed into specific aircraft requirements over individual segments of the network. For an individual firm, this methodology could suggest quantities of new model aircraft that should be purchased, optimal distribution of differing aircraft types over an integrated system, etc. For an over-all regulatory or planning agency, long-range needs of the system can be foreseen, and route award policy could be made with these in view.[1]

Section 1 presents an introduction to the examination of the 1957 figures. Section 2 contains some generally aggregate results, primarily in terms of over-all cost comparisons between the different models. In Section 3, values for the 1957 models are given a more comprehensive analysis. Section 4 deals with the results for 1963 in essentially the same way, whereas Section 5 explores some of the possible comparisons between the 1957 and 1963 figures. Section 6 contains a final summary.

1. Introduction

As a preface to this chapter, an attempt will be made to examine the predominant causes of discrepancies between the theoretically ideal solutions for the year 1957 and the actual observed solutions, i.e., the flight schedules that were in effect that year. It seems reasonable to suggest that, if the desire of airline industry officials or those in the regulatory agency were to provide a system which functioned at minimum total direct cost, then the model presented in this study would be a rational way of arriving at least at a first approximation to the allocation of airplanes. The constraints supply little more than an embodiment of logical and necessary technological restraints and conditions. Insofar, however, as other objectives weigh in the decisions of those concerned with this industry, the model may produce answers that are overly ideal.[2] If a *primary* interest is not exclusively in minimizing cost, i.e., in providing an efficient system, then of course the objective function itself may be called into question.[3] Several comments are in order; these points will be discussed in some detail in the following pages.

1. The model may still omit important features of the scheduling problems of the airlines. Some of these may be of such overwhelming

[1] This should be of particular interest to the CAB. "We have on many occasions pointed to the fact that our ultimate responsibility is to establish a sound air route system properly adapted to our national needs and that it would in the long run work a serious injury to the public interest if we were to give undue weight to the attainment of short-term objectives." *New York–Florida Case*, 24 CAB 94, 222 (1956).

[2] Cf. Marc Nerlove, "On the Efficiency of the Coal Industry," *Journal of Business*, XXXII (July, 1959), 271–278. This is a review of Henderson's study of the efficiency of the coal industry, using linear programming. It suggests caution when arguing from the results of a mathematical model (especially policy conclusions) which may embody basic assumptions that are unrealistic.

[3] Note that these arguments do not vitiate the use of the results of this model as a demonstration of the costs involved in having an inefficient system, whether or not that system is in any sense inevitable.

importance that, even if efficiency were the desire of both the CAB and all concerned airlines, it would still be inadequately handled by a model of the sort presented here. Internal airline equipment scheduling and routing problems come to mind here, as does the whole question of the uneven distribution of demand.

2. The airlines themselves may consider other factors in addition to least cost as equally if not more important, whether or not these are direct suggestions of the Board. The idea of developing potential demand would be one example.

3. The CAB itself may not directly encourage efficiency in this sense, and, in fact, may operate under a philosophy which is in some ways opposed to that goal. The idea of balanced competition is a case in point.

4. Other government agencies may have some priority and could thwart the efforts of the airlines and the CAB to provide an efficient system. The assignment of mail flights for the Post Office Department would theoretically qualify here.

Demand Distribution

Uneven distribution of demand over a given time period means that there will be a variability of actual load factors if flights are scheduled on a regular (e.g., daily) basis. Family fare plans and off-season excursion rates were introduced by the airlines to help combat this situation by redistributing demand more evenly over the various days of the week. Such plans have met with only limited success. One possible solution is for the airlines to schedule equipment irregularly to conform more closely to uneven demand. To some extent this is done, but complex scheduling considerations make this a less than perfect solution.

Perhaps some passenger inconvenience in the name of increased efficiency is not unreasonable.[4] The question of how far and how much

[4] An extremely efficient policy would be for an airline to stipulate that no flight shall leave the ground unless and/or until the load factor is greater than some pre-specified figure. Not only would such elastic scheduling probably lead to extremely negative public response, but it would also interfere with further scheduled use of equipment, and finally it would lead to difficult problems of air traffic control that now depends on published flight schedules for at least some element of regularity in arrivals and departures at any airport. Cf., however, *Aviation Week*, July 18, 1960, p. 52: "Eastern Air Lines' new program of strict scheduling of flights according to traffic demands in place of the former policy of high-rate frequency scheduling has resulted in the withdrawal of 31 piston-engine aircraft from active service and reduction of the company's personnel force by about 1,000 employees."

potential passenger demand should and does adapt to published airline schedules has already been discussed.[5] A different case, which was highlighted by the December, 1960, mid-air collision over New York City, is that increasing numbers of aircraft lead to magnified problems of air traffic control and safety. It might be argued that potential air travelers will accept some scheduling inconveniences in the name of increased efficiency if this implies fewer aircraft in the skies. Most airlines keep no records of passengers who were refused service because a particular flight was sold out. It is difficult to form an accurate picture of the distribution of demand within an operating day; for longer periods of time this becomes easier, and has to some extent been done.

Airline Equipment Routing

All airlines are concerned in some measure with achieving high equipment utilization. This implies, however, that although some segments of a route sequence (which consists of several consecutive hops) may frequently provide very low demands, the entire "loop" must be flown in order that equipment be available at high-demand nodes when scheduled. Such scheduling problems, from an individual airline viewpoint, could also be treated by a mathematical programming format.[6] These problems become less important for the current study because the concern here is with high-traffic nodes and nonstop flights between them. The influence of such considerations, however, is almost impossible to quantify in a large study involving several airlines, because for certain airlines on certain routes this may be an important factor, while for others the existence of more spares at critical points may render the consideration unnecessary.

[5] See pp. 74–77. Of course, if one argues the extreme case that the basic function of an airline system is to transport passengers at the times when they wish to go, then from the point of view of regulatory policy nothing should be done in this area. It is well to admit openly that no consideration of total welfare implications has been undertaken here. It may be that even if increased efficiency through reduced numbers of flights resulted directly in price decreases for the traveling public, there might still be a net loss in terms of total welfare of the passengers involved. People may be willing to pay a good deal for the convenience of choice among numerous departures.

[6] Cf., for example, Joseph F. McCloskey and Fred Hanssmann, "An Analysis of Stewardess Requirements and Scheduling for a Major Domestic Airline," *Naval Research Logistics Quarterly*, IV (September, 1957), 183–191, where the objective was to minimize "away from home time" for flight personnel given routes that required passenger service.

Potential Demand

In the programs of this study, concern has been focused on the most efficient transportation of particular numbers of passengers. In the 1957 model this was the number actually transported; in the 1963 model this was the projected number of people who will demand transportation. Airlines may tend to overschedule — in particular, to use newer, higher-capacity equipment — on those routes where it is felt that the provision of attractive service will induce more traffic.[7] If this proved to be a general phenomenon, one could adjust the actual and projected demand figures upward by some margin designed to reflect this total market (actual plus potential) for which optimum solutions are desired. In view of the lack of clear evidence that this is indeed general policy, such adjustments have not been made in this study. However, if practiced by only a few airlines over a few routes, this will contribute to the differences between actual figures and those generated by the model.

Balanced Competition

The basic idea behind the Board's position on competition is simply that the public stands to gain in terms of service when more than one carrier operates a given route. Appendix A has considered this facet of CAB policy. This attitude, in practice, has led to a rather large number of carriers on some routes.[8]

It is interesting to note that one basic argument in favor of the competition theory, namely, to provide more frequent schedules for cities formerly served by a single airline with necessarily limited aircraft, is weakened by the advent of higher-speed jet-prop and pure-jet equipment. By virtue of their speed potential alone, an airline is able to serve more nodes (or the same nodes more frequently) with a single airplane.[9]

[7] This apparently has not been encouraged by the Board, but it may nonetheless be standard policy at least for certain airlines on some routes. Cf. "Adequacy of Domestic Airline Service: The Community's Role in a Changing Industry," *Yale Law Journal*, LXVIII (May, 1959), 1234.

[8] In 1961, for example, New York–Washington was served by 10 carriers; New York–Chicago, 5; New York–Boston, 6; New York–Detroit, 6.

[9] The same jet equipment also renders less effective the argument against excessive competition among the airlines which rests on the fact of potential competition offered by other forms of transport: railroads, buses, and private automobiles. The increased time advantage introduced by such equipment is not easily offset, although generally increased fares on jets (for all classes of service offered) again give some price-competitive advantages to land transport.

It has been suggested that an economic constraint applies to the extent that when an additional airline is authorized to serve an already well-scheduled route, the new airline will not exercise its privilege unless there is clearly the demand to warrant additional service.[10] If this is the case, then most new airlines on any particular route seem to have been extremely optimistic in their assessment of existing or potential demand.

There is some evidence that the Board's position with regard to competition may be undergoing some critical reevaluation.[11] Any steps in the direction of a reduction of the numbers of carriers on individual routes would undoubtedly produce a more efficient system, as the results of this chapter will indicate. Until such time as concrete measures are taken, however, the results of a philosophy of balanced competition must be regarded as an important cause of differences between the ideal results of this study and actual observed scheduling.

Mail Flights

A reading of the statutes pertaining to the relations between the Post Office Department and the commercial airlines might leave one with the impression that many flights that are not profitable from the point of view of passengers carried are nonetheless dispatched in order to transport mail. This seems especially true between important business centers, where late afternoon air mail is expected to be delivered at its destination the following morning.

By provisions which existed in the Civil Aeronautics Act of 1938 and which have been included in the Federal Aviation Act of 1958, the Postmaster General may designate any published and scheduled flights as mail-carrying flights. Moreover, he has the power to require additional schedules for the transport of mail.[12] However, these broad powers are subject to review and final approval by the Civil Aeronautics Board. There seems to be an economic restraint as well. If it had been felt that adequate potential passenger traffic existed between the points in question at the time suggested, regular scheduled airline service would already have been instituted. Thus the Post Office De-

[10] Cf. United Research Incorporated, *Federal Regulation of the Domestic Air Transport Industry* (Cambridge: United Research Incorporated, 1959), pp. 44, 131.

[11] See the address of Alan S. Boyd, CAB Chairman, at the Connecticut General Symposium on "The Issues and Challenges of Air Transportation," Hartford, Connecticut, November 3, 1961.

[12] 72 *Stat.* 760 (1958), especially Section 1371 (m), 1375 (a), (b), (c), and (d).

partment, by insisting upon new schedules, would be encouraging a situation that could lead to the necessity for government subsidization through the mail pay provisions, and this is a consequence that the Post Office Department might find untenable.[13] It therefore appears that consideration of flights necessary for the transport of mail should not play any role in explaining discrepancies between ideal and actual allocations.

2. General Results and Comparisons

Measures of Aggregate Cost

Figures for total cost of each of the models provide several bases for comparison. In the 1957 intercity model that assumed 95 per cent capacity throughout the nine-node system, total demands were satisfied at a total weekly cost of $2.7 million. The same model with 60 per cent capacity assumed involved a total cost of $4.2 million.[14] These figures may be compared with a total cost, in terms of flights actually operating over the routes in question in 1957, of $9.1 million.[15] Even if the 95 per cent formulation is discarded as too far removed from reality, the total cost of the system was over twice what it need have been.[16]

[13] The fact that currently all domestic trunklines are off government mail subsidy suggests that the Postmaster General has not used this power. The development of coach travel (especially late night departures), all cargo flights using hours of low traffic density, and the shrinking of flying time between major cities because of high-speed jet aircraft have all helped bring about a coincidence of Post Office desired departure hours and airlines' scheduling.

[14] These costs take into account the fact that solution variables have been rounded to the next highest integer. That is, they are the rounded numbers multiplied by relevant cost parameters and then summed. The differences between the optimum value of the objective function in each of these continuous models and its augmented counterpart are given in the following table, where the figures are thousands of dollars:

	1957				1963			
	Intercity		Interregional		Intercity		Interregional	
	95%	60%	95%	60%	95%	60%	95%	60%
Continuous	2,611	4,192	3,208	5,053	3,978	6,400	5,705	9,812
Rounded Upward	2,709	4,230	3,239	5,110	4,039	6,467	5,750	9,876

[15] The numbers of flights operating in 1957 are available in monthly issues of *Official Airline Guide* for that year. The costs by which they were multiplied are those in the objective function of the models used in this study.

[16] This is apparently a more striking result than is usually found in applied linear programming problems. See Robert Dorfman, "Operations Research," *American Economic Review*, L (September, 1960), 617: ". . . the usual upshot of a linear programming analysis or a transportation problem study is to find a plan that will reduce costs by 2 or 3 or 5 per cent."

For the interregional network in 1957, the results also indicate inefficiency. The 95 per cent model assigns a cost of $3.2 million to the total operation; the 60 per cent model requires $5.1 million; actual cost for this composite system in 1957 was $10.8 million. Again the actual cost is more than twice the 60 per cent value. Later, in Section 3, these costs of overscheduling are distributed over the routes on which they occurred.

An important logical point that now arises is the following: What is the explanation for the differences and discrepancies between the 1957 model results assuming a 60 per cent load factor and the actual figures for 1957, a year in which the over-all load factor was asserted to be around 60 per cent?

Although the trunkline industry over-all load factor for 1957 may be recorded as close to or approximately 60 per cent, this is for all lines and over all routes. The conclusions on pp. 115–118 suggest that costs of overscheduling are directly related to both distance between nodes and to demand. Since this study deals with a large number of high-density, long-haul routes, it is not unexpected that the figures for actual costs are high.

Moreover, the models used in this analysis assign the best or most appropriate aircraft to each route; i.e., it is not only the load factors that must be the same for the costs to be approximately the same, the same equipment must be used over the same routes.

For example, in the 60 per cent model, 8 CV-340's carry 200 passengers, as do 5 DC-6B's. In the 200 to 400 mile range, the Convairs cost 66 cents per airplane mile, the Douglas aircraft cost 79 cents. Thus, to carry 200 people on Convairs costs 8 × (0.66) = $5.28 per mile; on the Douglas planes the cost would be 5 × (0.79) = $3.95 per mile. Admittedly, if the DC-6B's are scarce, then they must be used where the range of Convairs (for example) is too short. And this would show up in a model in which capacity constraints were exhausted. As will be discussed later, this was not the general rule in the programs of this study. The example also suggests that figures for operating costs per airplane-mile, by stage lengths, do not say too much about total economies. Total demand involved is also very important, i.e., the numbers of people who must be transported over the stages in question.

For the present, attention will continue to be focused on over-all figures. Two further measures are given which indicate the magnitude of the inefficiency in the 1957 system and which will be of use when the 1963 results are presented for comparison. The first is cost per passenger, which results from dividing total number of passengers accommodated within the system into total costs. In the 1957 intercity model, there was a total of 152,610 individual demands that were met. In the 1957 interregional model, this total was 132,770, somewhat less.[17] Costs per passenger are shown in Table 6-1.

TABLE 6-1. 1957 COSTS PER PASSENGER

(Dollars)

Intercity Model:	
95 per cent	17.75
60 per cent	27.72
Actual	59.75
Interregional Model:	
95 per cent	24.40
60 per cent	38.49
Actual	81.40

In addition to focusing attention again on the high actual costs in 1957, these figures also reflect the fact that the aggregate model spans a much larger geographical area. They therefore suggest a further measure of airline costs which will be employed: cost per passenger-mile. The number of passengers carried over a given route is multiplied by the length of that route to give passenger-miles produced.[18] Total passenger-miles, over all routes, divided into total system cost gives cost per passenger-mile. These are presented in Table 6-2.

TABLE 6-2. 1957 COSTS PER PASSENGER-MILE

(Dollars)

Intercity Model:	
95 per cent	0.0202
60 per cent	0.0315
Actual	0.0679
Interregional Model:	
95 per cent	0.0197
60 per cent	0.0311
Actual	0.0654

[17] New nodes are added to the interregional model, but at the same time much intraregional traffic, which formerly comprised several different routes, is now obscured.

[18] E.g., four passengers on a 1,500-mile route equal 6,000 passenger-miles. The 1957 and 1957 aggregate models contain 134.3 million and 164.3 million passenger-miles, respectively.

Again the inefficiency of actual 1957 scheduling is clear. In addition, however, the costs in the interregional model indicate decreases relative to those in the intercity model. An improvement in the relative position of the interregional model occurs when due accord is given to the fact that a greater total distance is covered, although fewer passengers are included in the regional formulation. Consideration of both numbers of passengers and also distances involved becomes especially important when geographically different systems are compared.

For the 1963 formulation there are as yet no "actual" figures — allocations and consequent costs — against which to set the theoretical results. However, because essentially the same geographic sets were used in both the 1957 and the 1963 models, with only the individual demands and the aircraft types changed, some interesting comparisons are possible.[19] For 1963, the intercity model included 277,800 passengers and 263.1 million passenger-miles; the interregional model had 293,000 passengers and 375.9 million passenger-miles. Comparable cost data for 1963 are shown in Table 6-3.

TABLE 6-3. 1963 COST DATA
(Dollars)

	Total Cost	Cost per Passenger	Cost per Passenger-Mile
Intercity Model:			
95 per cent	4,039,000	14.54	0.0154
60 per cent	6,467,000	23.28	0.0246
Interregional Model:			
95 per cent	5,750,000	19.63	0.0153
60 per cent	9,876,000	33.71	0.0263

Table 6-4 is provided to facilitate comparisons. It reveals that both cost per passenger and cost per passenger-mile decline in the 1963 model, relative to their 1957 counterparts. This is consistent with manufacturers' claims and purchasers' hopes that the greater capacity and speed of new-model jet aircraft would make them inherently more economical transport vehicles.

In 1957, the costs per passenger-mile were somewhat lower in the interregional model than in the intercity one. In the 1963 results, this was true for the 95 per cent model, although the difference was

[19] Cleveland was not included in the 1963 intercity model.

very small, but not for the 60 per cent model. If total passenger-miles are used as a measure of relative system size, this indicates that trunklines should be able to serve large new blocks of long-haul demand at no increase and perhaps even a decrease in unit cost per passenger-mile.

TABLE 6-4. COST FIGURES FOR COMPARISON
(All figures in dollars)

	1957		1963	
	Cost per Passenger	Cost per Passenger-Mile	Cost per Passenger	Cost per Passenger-Mile
Intercity Model:				
95 per cent	17.75	0.0202	14.54	0.0154
60 per cent	27.72	0.0315	23.28	0.0246
Interregional Model:				
95 per cent	24.40	0.0197	19.63	0.0153
60 per cent	38.49	0.0311	33.71	0.0263

These figures could be used to support the following proposal for organization of a domestic air transport system. The country should perhaps be divided into a relatively small number of composite nodes. These would generate large amounts of traffic to other such nodes, and they would exhaust the major geographical regions of the country. Then, the argument would run, all demand between these composite nodes should be handled by trunklines with long-haul, high-speed, and high-capacity equipment. Movement of passengers within the nodes themselves should be left to local service airlines with generally smaller-capacity, lower-speed equipment. In this way an extremely efficient system would result.[20] More important, perhaps, from the practical point of view is that any movement in this direction would be desirable.

Aircraft Use and Economies

Both the 1957 and the 1963 models were perhaps overly generous in aircraft availability allowances. They included *all* aircraft of the types considered which were owned by the participating trunklines in the 1957 model. For 1963, they were based on estimates of total domestic airline purchases. To have estimated, in some way, the

[20] The fact that the Board conceives of trunklines and local service airlines as fulfilling two different purposes and therefore having roles as noncompeting suppliers was recently reiterated in an initial decision in the *Pacific–Southwest Local Service Case*. See report in *Aviation Week*, February 13, 1961, pp. 39–40.

proportion of each airline's fleet which was or would be in use over the system considered would be almost impossible for 1963, and for 1957 it would have involved an improper assumption. It would have meant acceptance of the airlines' allocations of aircraft over individual routes, and these need not necessarily have been efficient.

Inclusion of all aircraft, however, had the result that in only two of the eight programs were one or more aircraft types used to capacity. In general, only one aircraft type was employed on any given route in the ideal allocations, and thus most of the results presented in this chapter have been aggregated over aircraft types for each route. Note that this can distort the comparison of flights assigned over a particular route but that it will not influence cost figures. If in actuality 116 Viscount flights were scheduled between Chicago and Washington, for example, but the theoretical model assigned 104 DC-6B's and 12 DC-3's, the total flights would be the same. There does not appear to be any satisfactory way of weighting flights of various sorts of aircraft in terms of one other aircraft type. Since the actual cost figures for each route in each problem are aggregates of the products of each type of aircraft flight observed and its corresponding cost, this problem is not carried over into the comparative cost figures.

The results of the 1957 model were consistent with a historical fact of piston aircraft economics. For in very few cases — generally because of nonstop range limitations — was airplane type 1 used; in almost all others type 2 was selected. Type 1 has the characteristics of the DC-7 and type 2 those of the DC-6B. From the cost point of view of this study there seems to have been little justification for the introduction of the DC-7. This has been noted by others:

> Thus we are back on the trend to lower unit cost [cost per available seat-mile] that was broken by the DC-7, which was the first plane ordered in quantity that had a higher operating cost than its predecessor.[21]

Indeed there may have been considerations other than increased luxury and speed — longer range was assuredly one of them — which encouraged the introduction of the DC-7, but the basic economic fact of higher unit costs has been reflected in this study.

Similarly, in the 1963 results, there is a strong tendency to favor type 2, this time exemplified by the Boeing 720. For at least two reasons

[21] A. M. deVoursney, "Airline Profits in the Jet Age," address before the Security Analysts of San Francisco, October 25, 1956, p. 5.

these results should be interpreted as less decisive. In the first place, the cost data for the 1963 airplane types rested heavily on predicted or expected operating costs. There was some catalogued experience with early models of the Boeing 707 which had been in use by domestic airlines, but none for the 720. The manufacturers' estimates, although modified before use in this study, may still have been generous to the aircraft. Second, the numerous versions of type 1 aircraft provide a rather wide area of available power, range, capacity, and consequently cost possibilities.[22] The categorization that was selected for this study may not have been fine enough to have captured adequately the differences between these aircraft.

3. 1957 Results

Flight Overscheduling

By the criteria suggested earlier, the 1957 air transport system connecting the subset of domestic nodes considered in this study was an inefficient one. Excessive numbers of flights were scheduled in 1957, with a consequent total cost which was at least twice that necessary to meet the demand existing at the time. Table 6-5 indicates weekly flight assignments. The first entry in each cell is actual number of flights scheduled (aggregated over all aircraft types); the second is the level given by the solution to the problem with 95 per cent capacity; the third is the level given by the solution to the problem with 60 per cent capacity.

Table 6-6 gives differences between actual and 60 per cent entries in Table 6-5. The results in both directions on the routes between New York and Miami, Chicago and Miami, and Boston and Miami deserve special attention. Negative values are recorded. That is, the actual assignments were better (involved fewer flights) than the linear programming model that assumed uniform 60 per cent load factors. Miami traffic is distributed unevenly but predictably over the twelve months of the year. By maintaining very flexible scheduling,[23] the

[22] There are basically four versions of the 707; the -120, -220, -320, and -420. These differ in capacity, range, and engine power. Moreover, all versions are now offered with turbofan engines, which apparently increase speed and economy, cut down noise, etc. The Douglas aircraft also come in several models. A probable new entrant by 1963 will be the Convair 900 (formerly designated the 600), which is larger and faster than the current Convair 880.

[23] Cf. the variation in monthly flight figures for these routes in any recent set of issues of the *Official Airline Guide*.

TABLE 6-5. WEEKLY FLIGHT ASSIGNMENTS, 1957
Actual, 95 per cent model, and 60 per cent model

FROM \ TO	New York	Chicago	Miami	Los Angeles	Washington	San Francisco	Detroit	Boston	Cleveland
New York		504	224	147	511	77	259	441	182
		143	145	61	101	40	52	115	43
		225	228	96	159	62	81	180	67
Chicago	504		70	238	175	126	259	98	133
	126		67	30	27	14	41	17	25
	197		105	47	43	22	65	26	39
Miami	224	70		*	91	*	42	21	28
	156	50			17		24	19	17
	246	78			26		38	30	26
Los Angeles	147	238	*		56	266	63	14	21
	55	32			13	132	10	9	6
	87	49			21	207	16	14	9
Washington	511	175	91	56		35	70	63	35
	101	25	17	14		11	12	19	13
	159	39	26	21		16	18	30	14
San Francisco	77	126	*	266	35		42	*	*
	40	17		126	11		6		
	63	26		199	18		9		
Detroit	259	259	42	63	70	42		14	133
	58	40	23	9	11	5		7	20
	93	62	35	14	17	7		10	31
Boston	441	98	21	14	63	*	14		42
	117	17	17	9	18		7		7
	185	27	27	14	28		10		11
Cleveland	182	133	28	21	35	*	77	42	
	44	24	16	6	12		20	7	
	69	37	25	10	13		32	11	

* Direct flights were not offered on these routes in 1957.

TABLE 6-6. FLIGHT ASSIGNMENT DIFFERENCES, 1957
Actual minus results from 60 per cent model

FROM \ TO	New York	Chicago	Miami	Los Angeles	Washington	San Francisco	Detroit	Boston	Cleveland
New York		279	−4	51	352	15	178	261	115
Chicago	307		−35	191	132	104	194	72	94
Miami	−22	−8		*	65	*	4	−9	2
Los Angeles	60	189	*		35	59	47	0	12
Washington	352	136	65	35		19	52	33	21
San Francisco	14	100	*	67	17		33	*	*
Detroit	166	197	7	49	53	35		4	102
Boston	256	51	−6	0	35	*	4		31
Cleveland	113	96	3	11	22	*	45	31	

* Direct flights were not offered on these routes in 1957.

actual load factor attained on these routes may well have been above the 60 per cent assumed in the model. In fact, on the Chicago to Miami, Miami to Boston, and Boston to Miami segments, the actual figures closely approach the 95 per cent solutions. The important element in all Miami traffic, and especially that to and from other large and important nodes, is the regularity and consequent predictability of the seasonal element.

These results are of interest in view of the relationship between air safety problems and increased numbers of aircraft in the skies. Especially over large demand centers, pile-up and stacking problems contribute significantly to this growing problem. Summing the entries in a given row in Table 6-6, provides an idea of the number of weekly flights (i.e., take-offs) that could be eliminated from any given air traffic node. Similarly, reading along any column indicates arrivals that might be eliminated.[24] In view of statements by Senator Monroney and the Senate Aviation Subcommittee which suggest that it may be necessary to limit arrivals and departures at certain high traffic centers in this country, these results (or results of a similar study for other

[24] These are particularly relevant figures, for ". . . more than 40 per cent of accidents happen during some phase of landing or take-off," *Aviation Week*, February 27, 1961, p. 41.

years) should be useful in indicating a logical way to distribute the arrival limitations over nodes of origin.[25]

In the remainder of this chapter, a number of tables of inversion counts will be presented. An inversion will be defined as occurring whenever an item in one ordered list is out of place vis-à-vis a second list, ordered according to some different criterion, by one ordinal place. That is, if the first item in one list is the third in the second list, two inversions are recorded.[26]

The general logic of the tables is as follows. An ordered list of deviations on each route (for example, actual flights minus theoretical assignments from the 95 per cent model) is compared with ordered lists of other magnitudes on the same routes, e.g., total demand and distance. Each list is headed by the route with the largest magnitude and ends with the route having the smallest number. Suppose that three such lists were as follows, where letters designate routes:

Flight Overscheduling	Total Demand	Total Distance
A	A	A
B	B	D
C	D	E
D	C	C
E	E	B

A count of inversions shows 1 in the demand column and 5 in the distance column, both as compared with the overscheduling list. These could then be presented in tabular form:

Flight Overscheduling	
Absolute Differences	
95 per cent model	
Demand	1
Distance	5
Total Possible Inversions: 10	

The two figures, when related to the total possible number of in-

[25] *Ibid.* The air safety problem is not one of numbers alone, of course. The crux of the matter lies in the bunching of demands and consequently of take-offs and landings. A reduction in the absolute numbers of aircraft on a given route would certainly not increase the safety problem, however, and it might contribute to decreasing it.

[26] These may be measured by assigning an ordered set of numbers to the items in one list and the same numbers to the (differently ordered) items in the second list and then counting the number of interchanges in the second list, or by placing the ordered columns side by side, connecting corresponding items by straight lines, and counting the number of intersections of such lines.

versions, indicate (in this example) that the relative tendency of high-demand routes to be overscheduled is stronger than the tendency for long-distance routes to be overscheduled.

In some cases, for reasons made specific as they are presented, these tables will include a column of Percentage Differences in addition to Absolute Differences. In these cases, the *same* ordered lists of demand and distance are compared with a list of flight overscheduling as measured by percentage differences rather than absolute differences, ordered by routes from largest to smallest. These are simply [(Actual − Theoretical)/(Theoretical)] × 100 for the same overscheduling data.

It should be noted that in any such listings of n items, the total possible number of inversions (corresponding to complete *inverse* order between the listings) is $n(n - 1)/2$. Thus, whenever a number of inversions greater than one-half the total possible is recorded, it may be concluded that the two listings in question would correspond more closely if one were completely reversed. In terms of the preceding example, if the distance column had been $\begin{matrix}\mathrm{E}\\ \mathrm{D}\\ \mathrm{A}\\ \mathrm{C}\\ \mathrm{B}\end{matrix}$, this corresponds to 8 inversions out of a possible 10, and it may be concluded that greater overscheduling is much more closely related to shorter distance. If the distance column were ordered from shortest to longest $\begin{matrix}\mathrm{B}\\ \mathrm{C}\\ \mathrm{A}\\ \mathrm{D}\\ \mathrm{E}\end{matrix}$, only 2 inversions are recorded.

Certain relationships between overscheduling and other market characteristics have emerged. These are interesting not only within the confines of this particular study but they might also indicate trends throughout the entire domestic air transport network, although the actual scope of this study was considerably smaller. In particular, there is a tendency for the routes with relatively high demands to exhibit the greatest amount of overscheduling. Consider an ordered list of city-pairs (i.e., of nondirected routes), ranging in order from that with the highest total demand to that with the smallest. Consider also the same set of routes ranked according to distance between the nodes involved. By comparing each of these lists in turn with an ordered list of overscheduled flights over the same routes, it is possible to note the following points:

1. In general, the *greater* the total demand between city-pairs, the greater the absolute amount of overscheduling.
2. In general, the *smaller* the intervening distance between city-pairs (i.e., the shorter the route), the greater the amount of overscheduling.

The actual figures are as shown in Table 6-7.

TABLE 6-7. INVERSION COUNTS, 1957 FLIGHT ASSIGNMENT OVERSCHEDULING

	Absolute Differences		Percentage Differences	
	95 per cent model	60 per cent model	95 per cent model	60 per cent model
Demand	129	163	282	284
Distance	312	333	289	284

Total Possible Inversions: 496

If the listing of distances is reversed — ordered from shortest to longest — the figures for absolute differences are then 184 and 163, respectively. This result is not very surprising, since for the nodes investigated in this study the shorter routes were usually the ones with the higher total demands. The important point is that overscheduling tends to follow the same pattern, i.e., to increase for increases in total demand. This suggests that, should the CAB at some time in the future wish to restudy some of its route award policies with an eye toward cutting down on the absolute numbers of flights scheduled, it would do well to begin with predominantly short-haul, high-demand routes. New routes and existing routes not considered in the study might also be ranked according to total demand as an aid in selecting those on which the tendency toward inefficiency would be strongest.

A final group of comparisons was made between flight overscheduling and number of competitors on the routes involved. The results shed additional light on the long-standing CAB policy of balanced competition. The Board has frequently argued that several competing airlines over a given route with reasonably high demand were to be preferred because of "product improvements" that resulted for the air traveler — i.e., food service, schedule times, introduction of newer models of aircraft, etc. It has always been tacitly recognized that this involved some duplication of schedules and consequent excess capacity over particular segments, but the benefits allegedly outweighed the disadvantages. In an early study, Gill and Bates questioned the soundness of this philosophy and introduced data to support their argument that after two or at most three competitors service begins to get worse and not better over the route in question. The results shown in Tables 6-8, 6-9, 6-14, and 6-15 (and also later when pricing practices are considered) suggest agreement with these findings and also with another important and more recent source.[27] Basic conclusions are the following:

1. The most competitive routes always exhibit a great deal of overscheduling; the more competitive the route, the worse this overscheduling becomes.
2. If variety (i.e., choice of flights) is a desired end of CAB action, then *at most* four competitors on a given route are sufficient to produce this result, and even routes with two airlines tend to be very overscheduled.
3. If airlines on any particular route calculate in terms of equal division of that market, plus an additional percentage "extra margin," then the size of this percentage margin tends to increase with the number of competitors.[28]

The following evidence supports these conclusions. Routes are divided into groups according to the number of airlines operating on each route in 1957.[29] The data are differences between the number of

[27] Cf. Frederick W. Gill and Gilbert L. Bates, *Airline Competition* (Cambridge: Harvard University Printing Office, 1949), esp. pp. 131–132; David W. Bluestone, "The Problem of Competition Among Domestic Trunk Airlines," *Journal of Air Law and Commerce*, XX (Autumn, 1953), 50–87, *passim.*

[28] Assume a route with five competitors. If total demand (known to these airlines) were such as to warrant 200 flights with equipment of a certain size, each airline might reason as follows: "We are entitled to 20 per cent of the total business, at least. Therefore we will provide 40 flights. Since it would be nice to have a somewhat higher participation in this market, however, we will schedule a few flights above these 40, perhaps an additional 12 (i.e., 30 per cent more)." If all five reason in this way, the total overscheduling will also be 30 per cent higher, i.e., it will be 260 instead of 200. This is roughly what the mean values in Table 6–8 show. They indicate, in addition, that as the number of competitors increases, the percentage overscheduled by each airline (if it acts in the manner described here) increases.

[29] From *Official Airline Guide*, July, 1957, pp. B9–B17. The numbers were as follows: (9) New York–Washington; (6) Detroit–Chicago; (5) Washington–Chicago, New York–Detroit, Chicago–New York; (4) Los Angeles–Chicago, Miami–New York,

flights assigned (under both the 95 per cent and the 60 per cent assumptions) and the actual schedules, measured in both absolute and percentage terms. In general, the former are of more interest from the point of view of action that might be taken to reduce the disparities. Table 6-8 presents the average (mean) values for the actual number of extra flights in each of the seven competitive groupings. These values in the Absolute Differences column are simply the total numbers of extra (overscheduled) flights for each group divided by the number of routes in that group. The data are all derived from the previous tables and regrouped according to the number of competing airlines on each route. The mean value in the Percentage Differences column is derived by taking total overscheduling in each route class and dividing by the total number of theoretical flights (i.e., the values given by the model) for that same class (and multiplying by 100).[30]

The ranges in Table 6-9 indicate greatest and least overscheduling on particular routes in each grouping, for both the absolute differences and also for percentage differences. For the ordinal ranges, 32 indicates the greatest difference and 1 indicates the smallest difference.

TABLE 6-8. EXTENT OF COMPETITION AND MEAN VALUE OF FLIGHT OVERSCHEDULING, 1957

Absolute Differences			Percentage Differences	
95 per cent model	60 per cent model	Number of Airlines	95 per cent model	60 per cent model
820	704	9	406	221
437	391	6	540	308
482	399	5	335	177
317	233	4	224	103
109	82	3	227	108
87	55	2	153	62
19	7	1	79	18

New York–Cleveland, New York–Boston, Washington–Boston; (3) Los Angeles–New York, San Francisco–Chicago, San Francisco–New York, Los Angeles–Washington, Los Angeles–Detroit, Chicago–Boston, San Francisco–Washington, Miami–Washington, San Francisco–Detroit, San Francisco–Los Angeles, Los Angeles–Cleveland, Washington–Detroit, Los Angeles–Boston, Miami–Boston, Detroit–Cleveland, Washington–Cleveland; (2) Miami–Detroit, Chicago–Cleveland, Miami–Chicago, Cleveland–Boston; (1) Detroit–Boston, Miami–Cleveland.

[30] Note that this is not an average of percentages; i.e., it is not the percentage for each route in a classification, summed, and divided by the number of routes in the class.

TABLE 6-9. EXTENT OF COMPETITION AND RANGE OF FLIGHT OVERSCHEDULING, 1957

Range: Cardinal					Range: Ordinal (32–1)			
Absolute Differences		Percentage Differences			Absolute Differences		Percentage Differences	
95 per cent model	60 per cent model	95 per cent model	60 per cent model	Number of Airlines	95 per cent model	60 per cent model	95 per cent model	60 per cent model
820	704	406	221	9	32	32	20	20
437	391	540	308	6	29	29	27	27
739–298	586–268	573–275	327–182	5	31–26	31–26	29–15	29–18
650–99	517–(−26)	668–49	396–(−5)	4	30–14	30–2	31–3	29–3
274–6	204–(−15)	713–17	425–(−26)	3	24–1	24–3	32–1	32–1
217–23	190–(−43)	500–20	282–(−23)	2	22–4	23–1	23–2	24–2
23–14	8–5	100	40–10	1	5–3	6–5	8–7	9–5

It is not completely unexpected that flights are relatively highly overscheduled on those routes over which many competing airlines operate. But the fact that such extreme excesses of overscheduling are achieved with but a few competitors (note the ranges in Table 6-9) point out that whatever benefits are thought to accrue from variety in scheduling must become evident with at most four competitors. More than this number gives cause to question the soundness of CAB policy.[31]

In order to examine these results in a different manner, a multiple regression study was made. The object was to explain the overscheduling on each route (in terms of differences between actual flights in 1957 and those assigned in the 60 per cent model) by means of a linear function involving (1) number of competitors, (2) total demand, and (3) route distance. If these variables are represented by X_1, X_2, and X_3, respectively, where Y is the number of flights overscheduled, the resulting least-squares equation is

$$\begin{array}{l} Y = -78.3433 + 84.6375X_1 + 0.0074X_2 - 0.0440X_3 \\ \qquad\qquad\qquad (13.5) \qquad\qquad (0.0805) \qquad (0.0249) \end{array}$$

The numbers in parentheses are standard deviations of the regression coefficients. They indicate that the influence of the number of competitors X_1 is clearly significant. The effect of distance X_3 is less so, since the value of the regression coefficient is within the range that would be defined by two standard deviations around a mean of zero. That is, it is possible that the true regression coefficient could be zero. The effect, finally, of demand X_2 is clearly not significant. These

[31] It also casts doubt on such defense of Board action as is illustrated by the following statement (by a former Board member): "The growth in the volume of traffic on important routes has been accompanied by a steadily increasing volume of service, often by two or more carriers. Competition thus controlled has not resulted in increasing the capacity of the industry beyond the prospective demand for air transportation, but it has served to increase the quality and quantity of service offered and to stimulate the development of air traffic," Oswald Ryan, "Economic Regulation of Air Commerce by the States," *Virginia Law Review*, XXXI (March, 1945), 517–518. Another source puts the facts somewhat more candidly, and this points out clearly at least one consequence of the Board's policy of authorizing competitive services: ". . . one of the inherent problems of air transport operations is the fact that the minimum unit of production is substantially larger than the unit of sale. With competition, this factor becomes particularly critical. Assuming that each competitive carrier on a segment is aggressively seeking to preserve its relative share of the market, and therefore to provide its proportionate share of capacity, the action of one carrier to increase service would normally be accompanied or followed by similar action by the other carriers." See Exhibit No. AA–13, "Testimony of Melvin A. Brenner," American Airlines, Vol. VIII, p. 9, in *General Passenger Fare Investigation*.

findings parallel those indicated by the analysis of inversion counts, but they put them on a more rigorous basis.

The coefficient of multiple correlation $\bar{R}$, equals 0.78. Testing for the significance of $\bar{R}$ produces the variance analysis given in Table 6-10.

TABLE 6-10. VARIANCE ANALYSIS

1957 60 per cent model

	Degrees of Freedom	Sums	Mean Squares
Variance among Computed Values	3	718,732	239,577
Deviations of Observed from Calculated Values	28	276,676	9,881

The first value in the Sums column is the sum of squares of the deviations of computed values of Y from the mean value of Y. If there is actually no relation between flight overscheduling and the three variables selected, then this sum, divided by the relevant degrees of freedom, would provide an estimate of the variations in Y due solely to chance. On the other hand, if a relationship does exist between Y and the variables X_1, X_2, and X_3, the variations of Y about its mean will also include the influence of these factors and thus will be greater than if only chance were responsible.

The second entry in the Sums column is the square of the sums of deviations of observed from computed values of Y. This figure, divided by the appropriate degrees of freedom, is an estimate of the error variance.

The first variance is denoted by s_1^2, the second by s_2^2. Then $F = s_1^2/s_2^2$, and the logic of the F test should be clear. The null hypothesis under test is that both variances are estimates of the same quantity, the influence of chance effects on overscheduling. Put another way, the test is that there is no correlation between Y and the composite of factors represented by X_1, X_2, and X_3. In the present case, $F = 239{,}577/9{,}881 = 24.2$. Reference to standard tables indicates that for 3 degrees of freedom in the numerator and 28 in the denominator, $F_{.95} = 2.95$ and $F_{.99} = 4.57$. Thus even the 1 per cent figure is exceeded, and it may be concluded that the coefficient of multiple correlation is significant.[32]

[32] This is standard statistical analysis. See, for example, Frederick C. Mills, *Statistical Methods* (3rd ed., New York: Henry Holt & Co., Inc., 1955), pp. 612–656.

TABLE 6-11. COSTS OF FLIGHT ASSIGNMENTS, 1957

Actual, 95 per cent model, and 60 per cent model

(Thousands of dollars)

FROM \ TO	New York	Chicago	Miami	Los Angeles	Washington	San Francisco	Detroit	Boston	Cleveland
New York		342	341	518	123	290	132	87	87
		126	193	183	26	125	32	25	22
		198	303	288	41	193	50	40	34
Chicago	342		165	575	107	329	62	117	42
	111		96	64	20	32	11	18	9
	173		151	100	31	50	18	27	14
Miami	341	165		*	112	*	69	39	45
	207	72			19		35	29	22
	262	112			29		55	47	34
Los Angeles	518	575	*		190	132	171	53	63
	165	68			37	54	24	28	15
	261	104			59	85	38	44	22
Washington	123	107	112	190		128	37	26	14
	26	18	19	39		33	6	9	3
	41	28	29	59		49	9	14	4
San Francisco	290	329	*	132	128		102	*	*
	125	38		52	33		15		
	197	59		82	55		23		
Detroit	132	62	69	171	36	102		9	16
	36	11	33	21	6	13		5	3
	58	17	51	33	9	18		8	4
Boston	87	117	39	53	26	*	9		11
	26	18	26	28	9		5		5
	41	28	42	44	13		8		7
Cleveland	87	42	46	63	14	*	10	11	
	22	9	21	15	3		3	5	
	35	14	33	25	3		4	7	

* Direct flights were not offered on these routes in 1957.

Costs of Overscheduling

For a regulatory agency charged with providing an efficient system, an equally relevant set of data would refer to cost differentials, i.e., to the added costs due to overscheduling on particular routes. The data in Tables 6-11 and 6-12 are arranged in a manner analogous to Tables 6-5 and 6-6. The first presents total cost figures for particular routes, in thousands of dollars, for actual allocations and those in the 95 per cent and 60 per cent models. The second lists deviations — actual minus 60 per cent figures.

TABLE 6-12. DIFFERENCES IN COSTS OF FLIGHT ASSIGNMENTS, 1957

Actual minus results from 60 per cent model

(Thousands of dollars)

FROM \ TO	New York	Chicago	Miami	Los Angeles	Washington	San Francisco	Detroit	Boston	Cleveland
New York		144	38	230	81	97	82	47	53
Chicago	169		14	476	76	279	44	90	28
Miami	79	53		*	82	*	14	−7	10
Los Angeles	257	472	*		131	47	133	9	41
Washington	81	79	82	131		80	23	12	11
San Francisco	94	270	*	50	74		79	*	*
Detroit	75	45	19	138	28	84		1	12
Boston	46	89	−2	9	13	*	1		3
Cleveland	52	28	12	38	11	*	16	3	

* Direct flights were not offered on these routes in 1957.

This study has suggested that a least-cost definition is relevant for the efficiency question facing a regulatory body. For other types of analysis, the absolute number of flights might be more useful, especially when certain types of aircraft are available only in limited quantities.[33]

An inspection of orderings of absolute and percentage *cost* differences with routes ranked by demand and by distance points in the direction that has been suggested; costs of overscheduling are much more related to distance than are flights. This reflects the increase of

[33] E.g., if a country needed to borrow commercial aircraft for military uses during a wartime situation or when confronting an airlift problem, such as Berlin in the early days following World War II or the late-1960 Belgian airlift from the Congo.

total costs associated with longer routes. The results are shown in Table 6-13.

To extend, as before, to parts of a system which were not included in this analysis, or to time periods other than the particular one under study, distance between city-pairs may be considered *directly* related to the costs of overscheduling (not inversely, as was the case with numbers of flights) and the same is true for demand. Long-haul routes would come under closer scrutiny in such cases.

TABLE 6-13. INVERSION COUNTS, 1957 COSTS OF OVERSCHEDULING

	Absolute Differences		Percentage Differences	
	95 per cent model	60 per cent model	95 per cent model	60 per cent model
Demand	170	183	275	286
Distance	148	189	234	261
	Total Possible Inversions: 496			

A consideration of the interplay between costs of overscheduling and number of competitors involved leads to a stronger result than in the case of flights: With four competitive airlines the worst excesses of added cost are in evidence. Tables 6-14 and 6-15 show this.

TABLE 6-14. EXTENT OF COMPETITION AND MEAN VALUE OF OVERSCHEDULING COSTS, 1957
(Thousands of dollars)

Absolute Differences			Percentage Differences	
95 per cent model	60 per cent model	Number of Airlines	95 per cent model	60 per cent model
193	162	9	367	196
102	89	6	465	260
279	214	5	239	116
317	244	4	225	121
212	169	3	276	141
77	41	2	117	39
27	12	1	83	21

In the present case it seems extremely dangerous to imply that competition is solely responsible for these results. Rather, the figures may simply reflect the fact that routes with 9, 6, and 5 competitors are both highly competitive and also relatively short-haul. And this, in turn, is but a reflection of the fact that the CAB's policy of parallel route awards is somewhat more closely governed by the demand

TABLE 6-15. EXTENT OF COMPETITION AND RANGE OF OVERSCHEDULING COSTS, 1957

Range: Cardinal					Range: Ordinal (32–1)			
Absolute Differences*		Percentage Differences			Absolute Differences		Percentage Differences	
95 per cent model	60 per cent model	95 per cent model	60 per cent model	Number of Airlines	95 per cent model	60 per cent model	95 per cent model	60 per cent model
193	162	367	196	9	22	22	21	19
102	89	465	260	6	13	15	24	24
464–177	329–155	466–196	259–89	5	29–19	29–20	25–12	23–13
1,019–34	947–24	776–70	465–8	4	32–6	32–9	31–2	31–2
688–21	549–(−9)	842–42	508–(−11)	3	31–3	31–1	32–1	32–1
161–11	67–6	365–98	200–31	2	16–2	13–3	20–5	20–5
45–8	22–2	104–73	32–22	1	7–1	7–2	7–3	6–4

* In thousands of dollars.

characteristics of a particular route or network than it is by the distances involved.

Comparisons for the interregional problem using 1957 data reveal less certain results. The incidence of greatest overscheduling still seems to fall at the higher demand end of the scale, and in these cases costs are somewhat more closely associated with demand. This is in part a result of the fact that the aggregate nodes in the interregional model both obscure much of the traffic on high-density, short-haul, intranodal routes and also greatly magnify total (or one-way) demands on long-haul routes where both (or one) end points are aggregates. For example, San Francisco traffic with New York, Boston, Philadelphia, and Washington is now lumped together, along with traffic from Los Angeles to each of those points, on a long-distance route. Sixteen former cases of different-sized demands over eight long routes now become two cases of large demand over a single long route. Thus it is not unexpected that the cost-demand ordering is closer than in the intercity case. The data are presented in Table 6-16.

TABLE 6-16. INVERSION COUNTS, 1957 INTERREGIONAL MODEL

	Absolute Differences		Percentage Differences	
	95 per cent model	60 per cent model	95 per cent model	60 per cent model
		Flights		
Demand	29	42	75	76
Distance	56	61	63	64
		Costs		
Demand	28	38	78	80
Distance	41	37	53	62

Total Possible Inversions: 105

Shadow Prices

It is now appropriate to examine the solutions to the dual problems of each of the linear programs discussed thus far. These are an automatic by-product of the computations, and they are an interesting part of most problems. In Chapter 5, Section 1, economic interpretations for these dual variables were suggested briefly.

In any primal-dual programming relationship, the solution variables of one problem indicate changes in the value of the objective function of the second problem for a unit modification in the constraints of the second problem. In the present case, the solution of the dual problem is a set of *m* values, one for each activity in the dual (each constraint in the primal), indicating by how much the total cost function of the primal problem would *increase* if the right-hand side of the corresponding constraint in the primal were *increased* by one unit. Since the primal problem constraints read "greater than or equal to," this amounts to unit increases in the lower bounds to each constraint, i.e., making the requirements more severe.

In the programs of this study, there are three distinct groupings into which these dual variables fall. These will be discussed in turn; only the last of these three sets will be of specific interest.

Aircraft spares. The first set of constraints in the primal problem involves a balance condition on each aircraft type at each node. These inequalities state that any airport in the system may schedule no more departing flights of a given aircraft type to all other nodes than the sum of incoming flights of the same aircraft. Thus planes may pile up, but no spares are assumed at any node at the beginning of the operation. Clearly, the problem could be reformulated with any distribution of spares throughout the system that one wished to assume. The marginal costs involved here are the additional costs associated with increasing the spares minimum from zero to one at a given node, i.e., requiring that at least one aircraft stay at each node. Table 6-17 gives the figures for both 1957 intercity programs. The first figure is for the 95 per cent formulation, the second for the 60 per cent model; figures have been rounded to the nearest 10 dollars.

Relationships between primal and dual problems have been mentioned already.[34] The predominance of positive values for these variables means that the primal constraints are met with equality, i.e., that there is no piling-up of aircraft at most of the nodes. It happens that in fact every one of this first set of primal constraints is met with equality. That is, for those constraints with a zero price, the value of the slack variable in the associated constraint is zero, illustrating the fact that a zero-valued variable need not necessarily imply inequality in the corresponding constraint.

Aircraft time use. Since in no case was an availability constraint met with equality, the value or charge placed on the use of a particular type on any route remained at zero. It is for this reason that usually the most

[34] See p. 82.

TABLE 6-17. IMPUTED EQUIPMENT COSTS, 1957

95 per cent and 60 per cent models, respectively
(Dollars)

	Equipment Type			
	1	2	3	4
New York	820 800	880 880	880 880	530 520
Chicago	0 0	0 0	300 320	0 0
Miami	1,330 1,290	1,440 1,440	1,270 1,280	*
Los Angeles	1,650 1,660	1,840 1,840	0 0	0 0
Washington	690 670	730 730	780 790	460 450
San Francisco	2,080 2,020	2,250 2,250	270 250	210 200
Detroit	250 240	260 260	470 480	140 130
Boston	630 610	660 660	730 730	360 350
Cleveland	350 340	370 370	540 550	190 180

* Aircraft type 4 was never considered for any route to or from Miami because of nonstop range limitations.

efficient airplane type could be assigned to each route in the system; requirements were such that resort to second best was generally not necessary. In an expanded program, or in one with less generous aircraft availability constraints, at least some of these constraints might be expected to become equalities. Corresponding aircraft time would then become a nonfree good. This happens to some extent in the 1963 models and is discussed later.

Passenger travel prices. It is with the final and largest set of constraints that the economically most interesting results emerge. These imputed passenger travel prices, for both programs, are presented in in Table 6-18. As before, the first figure is for the 95 per cent model, the second for the 60 per cent model.

TABLE 6-18. IMPUTED PASSENGER TRAVEL PRICES, 1957
95 per cent and 60 per cent models, respectively
(Dollars)

FROM \ TO	New York	Chicago	Miami	Los Angeles	Washington	San Francisco	Detroit	Boston	Cleveland
New York		28	12	32	7	28	20	7	16
		44	20	51	10	44	31	11	25
Chicago	0		0	4	0	0	*	6	0
	0		0	7	0	0	*	10	0
Miami	30	46		43	29	55	41	37	38
	47	72		68	46	89	66	58	60
Los Angeles	63	63	56		62	0	63	69	63
	99	99	88		98	0	99	109	99
Washington	2	23	7	27		24	15	9	12
	3	37	10	43		38	24	14	19
San Francisco	71	71	77	13	72		71	81	71
	112	113	123	21	114		112	127	112
Detroit	0	8	4	13	*	8		6	*
	0	13	7	20	1	13		10	1
Boston	0	27	12	31	7	30	19		15
	0	43	19	50	10	48	30		24
Cleveland	0	12	4	16	*	11	4	6	
	0	19	6	26	1	18	6	10	

* Less than 50 cents.

First, it should be pointed out that in this case the entries with zero values correspond to primal constraints with negative slack variables, i.e., to situations wherein more capacity was dispatched over a given route than was necessary for the movement of passengers demanding transportation on that route. This occurred in order to maintain balance in the first set of constraints, the balance conditions. Logically, from the mathematical point of view, travel over the given route was classed as a free good in these cases. Second, it is clear here that the high incidence of positive values (and thus the large number of cases where dispatched capacity exactly meets demand requirements—i.e., equality constraints) is intimately connected with the continuous formulation of the program. Fractional planeloads are available to meet the extra amounts of demand. If an integer model were employed, this would also have effects on the values of these dual prices, other than making them integer-valued. In particular, many prices that are positive in this table might fall to zero.[35]

Table 6-19 presents differences between prices derived from the 60 per cent model and the actual 1957 first-class fares over the routes in question.[36] There is close correspondence between actual and model values in a number of cases. In many cases the airlines' pricing policies were apparently closer to a competitive ideal than might be supposed.

The same sort of inversion counts were performed here. In the present case the size of the price deviations (actual minus 60 per cent model) was ordered and compared with length of routes, size of demand, and number of competitors. For distance and demand, respectively, the counts were 51 and 317, out of a total possible 378. Thus the relationship of *longer* distance and overpricing is almost the same order of magnitude as *lower* demand and overpricing (51 and 61, respectively). The former is understandable insofar as longer routes have higher prices, and even a constant "percentage markup" would lead to relatively higher absolute deviations over longer routes.[37] The inverse relationship with demand may be partially only a reflection

[35] Ralph E. Gomory and William J. Baumol, "Integer Programming and Pricing," *Econometrica*, XXVIII (July, 1960), esp. 528–533 and 545–550, where the probable effects on the dual prices are treated in detail.

[36] In the case of the theoretical results, these are the average values of these prices for each route segment. That is, the sum of the prices in both directions, divided by 2. In the case of zero values (due to excess capacity, not rounding), the positive price in the opposite direction on the same route was used as the representative price and thus not divided. Note that there is no possibility of assigning excess capacity in *both* directions of any given route for any particular aircraft type.

Professor Benjamin Stevens has called attention to the fact that these prices reflect direct operating costs only; ground and indirect expenses are not included in the model. Had it been possible to consider these latter costs explicitly in the objective function of the primal problem, it is clear that the shadow prices in the dual would have been higher. Aircraft allocations could have been different as well; this would depend on the precise way in which indirect costs were apportioned among various aircraft. Note that the aggregate cost comparisons would be less affected, since the figures for actual 1957 costs employ parameters from the objective function of the model being used.

[37] With few exceptions, the percentage deviation is either very small (less than 10 per cent, for ten of the thirty-six segments) or very large (larger than 100 per cent, for the remaining twenty-six routes). With one exception (Chicago–Miami), the smaller percentages occur on relatively short routes.

TABLE 6-19. PRICE DIFFERENCES, 1957

Actual first-class fares minus figures for 60 per cent model

(Dollars)

Route		Differences
New York	– Chicago	1
	– Miami	43
	– Los Angeles	84
	– Washington	7
	– San Francisco	81
	– Detroit	0
	– Boston	1
	– Cleveland	1
Chicago	– Miami	8
	– Los Angeles	62
	– Washington	1
	– San Francisco	2
	– Detroit	3
	– Boston	27
	– Cleveland	1
Miami	– Los Angeles	75
	– Washington	35
	– San Francisco	67
	– Detroit	42
	– Boston	49
	– Cleveland	42
Los Angeles	– Washington	79
	– San Francisco	1
	– Detroit	70
	– Boston	88
	– Cleveland	74
Washington	– San Francisco	73
	– Detroit	14
	– Boston	14
	– Cleveland	11
San Francisco	– Detroit	67
	– Boston	80
	– Cleveland	69
Detroit	– Boston	20
	– Cleveland	4
Boston	– Cleveland	18

of the fact that, with few exceptions, the very long intercity routes are not ones with high demand. This has been noted on p. 108.

Investigation of competitive groups and overpricing is of more interest. The relevant data are presented in Table 6-20. Entries are differences of the 95 per cent and 60 per cent models, respectively, from actual.

TABLE 6-20. EXTENT OF COMPETITION AND PRICE DIFFERENCES, 1957

Mean Value			Range			
			Cardinal		Ordinal (28 − 1)	
95 per cent model	60 per cent model	Number of Airlines	95 per cent model	60 per cent model	95 per cent model	60 per cent model
9	7	9	9	7	4	6
8	3	6	8	3	3	4
14	1	5	17–11	1–0	8–6	2–1
34	24	4	81–5	62–1	20–1	17–2
67	53	3	118–6	88–1	28–2	28–2
30	17	2	56–8	42–1	18–3	14–2
41	31	1	54–27	42–20	17–12	14–11

The most immediate fact seems to be that there is a "threshold" number of competitors. Above this number the results that emerge strongly resemble those of purely competitive pricing, and below it large deviations are exhibited. In the present case this threshold number is four. Moreover, in the range between no competition (i.e., one airline) and four, there are interesting variants. The group consisting of three competing airlines has the generally largest overpricing policies (as measured by the mean value of the price deviations). Next in order are the routes served by one airline alone; this is followed by those with four and two competing lines, respectively.

In situations with more than four participating airlines, possibilities for effective collusive cooperation might be relatively small, and this would result in pricing not far from the competitive ideal, whereas fewer than that number would be able to act collectively and charge higher prices with some success. Moreover, the results in Table 6-20 cast serious doubt on the soundness of what appears to be the CAB position that two airlines are better than one and three are better still. In fact, from this point of view it would seem necessary to award each route to a relatively large number of airlines in order to assure anything approaching marginal cost pricing. These results are in agreement with a recent and thorough analysis of airline competition, one of the conclusions of which was that increased competition does not tend to decrease fares.[38] It runs somewhat counter to other recent works which assert that more vigorous price competition, with consequently lower fares, occurs on routes served by only one carrier.[39]

It should be mentioned that the actual factors involved in airline pricing decisions seem to be extremely varied from case to case. Moreover, rate making is not altogether free; it is controlled by the CAB. Airlines must file passenger rate schedules with the Board, which has the power to approve, suspend, or alter them.[40] Regardless of the factors that influenced particular price decisions, it is of interest to see the degree to which the results emulate the purely competitive ideal.

It must be remembered that the values obtained for the dual variables are dependent upon the original values in the problem; in this case the size of the various demands are decisive. Thus, as was emphasized earlier, the results here may not be taken to carry the authority of repeated experimentation. Models composed of different nodes and differing demands would be necessary before one could state with assurance that, for example, a route with fewer than five competitors is almost certain to be priced much above its attainable marginal cost ideal. But insofar as the foregoing results point in this direction, they indicate an interesting area of investigation and also an approach to the questions posed.[41]

For the interregional model, where composite routes do not allow

[38] Bluestone, *op. cit.*

[39] John Meyer, M. J. Peck, John Stenason, and Charles Zwick, *The Economics of Competition in the Transportation Industries* (Cambridge: Harvard University Press, 1959), esp. p. 230; Paul W. Cherington, *Airline Price Policy: A Study of Domestic Airline Passenger Fares* (Boston: Harvard University, Graduate School of Business Administration, 1958), p. 160.

[40] Sections 403 and 404 of the Civil Aeronautics Act set forth the responsibilities of the individual airlines for establishing and maintaining just and reasonable fares. Initiating and filing fares is a carrier responsibility. The Board's powers to alter such fares, should it find them unjust and unreasonable, are set forth in Section 1002 (d) through (h). The issue of airline pricing policies and a history of CAB responses to particular actions are discussed thoroughly in Cherington, *op. cit.*

[41] These results also are in a rather opposite direction from those for overscheduling and consequent costs. In those cases, an increase in the number of competitors usually was associated with an increased amount of overscheduling. However, insofar as the threshold number appears in the pricing analyses to be four, it would

classification by competitive group, the number of inversions for demand and distance (when compared with absolute amount of overpricing) was 38 and 41 of a total possible 105. This is relatively less decisive than the association exhibited in the intercity study. Furthermore, it reflects the tendency, already noted, for large demand to become attached to longer distance routes in the regional models.

4. 1963 Results

The solutions to the 1957 models made it possible to compare theoretical and observed results. For 1963, interest is centered on the use of such models as planning devices that, given the demand projections and equipment types available for some future time period, indicate what would be efficient flight assignments. Furthermore, the dual prices indicate ideal pricing policies under new equipment and demand conditions. With the exception of items noted later in this section, these results are primarily of interest when compared with the 1957 models, e.g., total costs and shadow prices on individual routes. These form the subject matter of the next section.

A new feature of the 1963 models is that some of the aircraft types were completely used up by the system. Some availability constraints were met with equality, and consequently a price was attached to an hour's use of the aircraft involved. This also is reflected in the marginal cost figures for aircraft available as spares at particular nodes.

In the 1963 intercity models the total availability constraint for aircraft type 2 is met with equality, and a shadow price of \$165 per hour's use emerges as a consequence. Thus, in contrast to the results of the 1957 studies, one aircraft type becomes a nonfree good.[42] This quality

---

seem more reasonable to reduce competition on many routes (thereby reducing overscheduling) and control price rather than to encourage so large a number of airlines over each route (with consequent increases in extra flights) in order to achieve more equitable pricing. This assumes, of course, that efficiency is still a primary aim.

[42] If this were the result for an individual airline study (or for a regulatory agency with *complete* control over prices), these added costs could be equitably distributed over the traveling public by increasing fares on those routes where this type of aircraft was used. This could be done by (1) dividing total assumed capacity into the shadow price, giving cost per passenger per hour; and (2) multiplying this by travel time assumed on each route using the aircraft, giving cost per passenger for the route in question. In cases where the aircraft is not the only type assigned, the result of (2) should be reduced by multiplying it by the proportion of flights of the aircraft in question to total assigned flights.

shows itself clearly in the resulting equipment cost figures at different nodes. As before, the zero-valued items do *not* correspond to cases where constraints were met with inequality in the corresponding problem. No piling-up of aircraft occurs. As Table 6-21 indicates, type 2 is the only aircraft that has increased marginal costs at every (nonzero-valued) node.

TABLE 6-21. IMPUTED EQUIPMENT COSTS, 1963

95 per cent and 60 per cent models, respectively
(Dollars)

Node	Equipment Type 1	2	3	4
New York	6,420	4,010	2,867	530
	6,195	4,862	3,165	847
Chicago	4,610	2,880	2,287	190
	4,510	3,492	2,271	296
Miami	3,678	2,290	1,986	0
	3,871	2,777	1,805	0
Los Angeles	230	150	117	162
	130	181	119	126
Washington	5,989	3,730	2,733	428
	5,740	4,523	2,942	700
San Francisco	0	0	0	0
	0	0	0	0
Detroit	5,160	3,220	2,460	288
	4,940	3,905	2,539	459
Boston	5,960	3,720	2,637	350
	5,821	4,512	2,937	667

The supply of both aircraft types 2 and 3 was exhausted in the 1963 interregional model, and prices of $268 and $45, respectively, were assigned to an hour's use of their time. Table 6-22 shows that the shadow prices for both these aircraft types increased at all nodes, in contrast to the other two types which were available.

TABLE 6-22. IMPUTED EQUIPMENT COSTS, 1963 INTERREGIONAL MODEL

95 per cent and 60 per cent models, respectively

(Dollars)

	Equipment Type			
Node	1	2	3	4
1	5,543	4,090	2,151	2,586
	6,545	5,510	3,598	2,625
2	4,139	2,960	1,579	2,028
	4,738	3,988	2,608	1,915
3	4,221	2,370	1,271	2,076
	3,795	3,197	2,089	1,579
4	0	230	0	366
	367	311	207	166
5	0	0	0	0
	0	0	73	0
6	3,110	2,170	1,109	1,616
	3,477	2,927	1,913	1,416
7	4,933	3,300	1,742	2,346
	5,287	4,452	2,910	2,144

5. Particular Comparisons: 1957 and 1963

Costs

Since aircraft types are radically different in the two time periods selected, any comparisons of differences in the absolute numbers of flights scheduled in the two years under the assumption of first a 95 per cent and then a 60 per cent load factor would be of little interest. However, the increases in flights scheduled on each route under the latter assumption can be converted to dollar terms by multiplying by the relevant cost figures. Thus it is possible to indicate the increase in costs for a particular segment when the system moves from a perfectly ideal, 95 per cent load factor scheduling to one with 60 per cent. Tables 6-23 and 6-24 show these increases in costs for individual routes for the two years, for the intercity and interregional models, respectively. Figures are in thousands of dollars.

These tables demonstrate, with only one exception in each case, that the introduction of assumptions of larger demand and larger-capacity aircraft raises the costs of inefficiency over all routes in question. In

TABLE 6-23. COST INCREASES, 95 PER CENT MODEL VS. 60 PER CENT MODEL ALLOCATIONS: 1957 AND 1963 (INTERCITY)

(Thousands of dollars)

Route		1957 Cost Increase	1963 Cost Increase
New York	– Chicago	135	220
	– Miami	165	410
	– Los Angeles	201	351
	– Washington	30	47
	– San Francisco	140	206
	– Detroit	40	78
	– Boston	29	50
Chicago	– Miami	95	109
	– Los Angeles	72	158
	– Washington	22	42
	– San Francisco	38	44
	– Detroit	12	17
	– Boston	20	36
Miami	– Los Angeles	13	32
	– Washington	20	36
	– San Francisco	9	19
	– Detroit	38	62
	– Boston	33	68
Los Angeles	– Washington	42	87
	– San Francisco	61	84
	– Detroit	26	21
	– Boston	35	65
Washington	– San Francisco	36	78
	– Detroit	6	8
	– Boston	10	24
San Francisco	– Detroit	13	29
	– Boston	21	36
Detroit	– Boston	5	9

terms of costs of total system inefficiency, it can be expected that as long as actual assignments remain less optimal than the 60 per cent model solutions, these costs will increase markedly. That is, the need for some method of efficient scheduling over an integrated system will become greater in the years to come.

Pricing

Interesting results emerge when the dual prices are considered. In Section 3 shadow prices for the movement of individuals were

TABLE 6-24. COST INCREASES, 95 PER CENT MODEL VS. 60 PER CENT MODEL ALLOCATIONS: 1957 AND 1963 (INTERREGIONAL)

(Thousands of dollars)

Route	1957 Cost Increase	1963 Cost Increase
1–2	353	546
–3	313	907
–4	525	1,311
–5	60	119
–6	42	80
–7	29	49
2–3	151	235
–4	189	317
–5	21	272
–6	18	26
–7	18	19
3–4	19	44
–5	0	9
–6	3	12
–7	17	19
4–5	62	95
–6	20	43
–7	7	12
5–6	2	3
–7	0	7
6–7	3	2

presented as a purely competitive ideal. What might happen to these prices (and in consequence, perhaps, the prices that actually will be established in the future) under the different assumptions of the projective model? The aircraft used in the 1963 model have distinct capacity and time advantages over those of the 1957 study. Will these be overshadowed, however, by the higher costs per airplane-mile which obtain in all cases of jet equipment?

Tables 6-25 and 6-26 shed light on these questions. The first concerns the intercity models, and the second deals with interregional models. The first column of figures in each table is the shadow price arrived at in the 1957 60 per cent model, averaged over both directions for each route. This is the more realistic price from the standpoint of actual airline pricing. The second column contains the same data for the 1963 case. In the third column, differences are recorded, where

TABLE 6-25. INTERCITY 60 PER CENT MODEL PRICES, 1957 AND 1963, AND DIFFERENCES

(Dollars)

Route		1957 Model	1963 Model	Difference (1963 – 1957)
New York	– Chicago	44	40	–4
	– Miami	34	61	27
	– Los Angeles	75	68	–7
	– Washington	7	6	–1
	– San Francisco	78	71	–7
	– Detroit	31	14	–17
	– Boston	11	10	–1
Chicago	– Miami	72	33	–39
	– Los Angeles	53	96	–43
	– Washington	37	17	–20
	– San Francisco	113	51	–62
	– Detroit	13	12	–1
	– Boston	27	24	–3
Miami	– Los Angeles	78	71	–7
	– Washington	28	51	23
	– San Francisco	106	84	–22
	– Detroit	37	33	–4
	– Boston	39	35	–4
Los Angeles	– Washington	71	64	–7
	– San Francisco	21	10	–11
	– Detroit	60	54	–6
	– Boston	80	72	–8
Washington	– San Francisco	77	69	–8
	– Detroit	13	11	–2
	– Boston	12	11	–1
San Francisco	– Detroit	63	113	50
	– Boston	88	79	–9
Detroit	– Boston	20	18	–2

a *positive* value indicates an *increase* in these prices between the 1957 and 1963 models.

The absence of large increases and, in fact, the predominance of negative values are striking, especially in the intercity case. This result suggests that in a competitive pricing situation, the traveling public would generally benefit from reduced fares which the economies of jet aircraft should make possible. In 1957 there were no segments

TABLE 6-26. INTERREGIONAL 60 PER CENT MODEL PRICES, 1957 AND 1963, AND DIFFERENCES

(Dollars)

Route	1957 Model	1963 Model	Difference (1963 – 1957)
1–2	22	22	0
–3	67	67	0
–4	75	76	1
–5	80	160	80
–6	42	42	0
–7	23	24	1
2–3	72	37	–35
–4	106	107	1
–5	115	116	1
–6	24	25	1
–7	36	18	–18
3–4	78	79	1
–5	89	90	1
–6	41	41	0
–7	36	18	–18
4–5	30	30	0
–6	76	76	0
–7	60	60	0
5–6	52	52	0
–7	71	72	1
6–7	23	23	0

for which the actual established first-class price was lower than these model prices, although in numerous cases the actual prices were not a great deal higher. Since the 1963 model has demonstrated the feasibility of generally lower prices throughout the system, it may be concluded that any price increases occurring between 1957 and 1963 will tend to move the air transport industry further away from its purely competitive ideal in terms of prices charged.[43] Moreover, insofar as the cost data used in this study include an equipment depreciation allowance, the fact of much higher individual aircraft costs in the case of the jets has been incorporated in these models.

[43] There has already been one general increase (late 1960) following the CAB's opinion in the *General Passenger Fare Investigation*.

6. Summary

In view of the number of conclusions and the various interpretations of results that are included in this final chapter, it seems advisable to recapitulate to some extent. Numbers will be avoided at this point, and attention will be concentrated on qualitative statements.

Comparison of over-all cost per passenger-mile figures for intercity and interregional programs in both years showed that the increased demands projected for 1963 can be accommodated at reduced costs over the routes in question with the aircraft which should be operating at that time. This is a basic result of the economies inherent in the jet equipment, and it has implications for pricing policies, as will be suggested in this section.

Examination of the same cost measure for the two types of models for a given year reveals that only with the 60 per cent model in 1963 is the interregional model cost per passenger-mile greater than that for the intercity model. In the other cases the reverse is true. This observation leads to the speculation that the larger equipment might be concentrated on long-haul, nonstop runs between large-demand centers and that the transport of passengers to the nearest long-distance node be carried out by local service airlines with smaller and less costly equipment. Any movement toward scheduling equipment in this way would seem to move the system in the direction of efficiency.

Perhaps transcontinental Philadelphia traffic, for example, from Portland, Oregon, or Spokane, Washington, should be treated as follows: (1) "fed" first into the Seattle-Tacoma airport, which would be the logical northwest node; (2) flown nonstop on high-speed, long-range equipment to New York; (3) flown from there by a smaller local line to Philadelphia. This sort of network existed at the beginning of the period of introduction of jet aircraft, when these planes were used exclusively on long-haul, high-density routes. But to an ever-increasing degree this equipment is being introduced into frequent nonstop service on relatively sparse long- or short-haul segments.[44]

The growing air safety problem is related to the number of airplanes in the sky. Results of the 1957 study indicated, for each node involved, the absolute number of flights overscheduled (on a weekly

[44] Cf. Paul S. Cline, "Airline Scheduling, Route Patterns, and Sales," *Journal of Air Law and Commerce*, XXIII (Spring, 1956), 164–169. This article, written before jets came into service, predicted that only ten to twelve cities in the domestic United States should be served by jets of the 707 or DC-8 class.

basis) for that year. This information, which categorizes the overscheduling into both departures from and also arrivals at the particular nodes in the study, would be of interest if, for example, New York and Chicago were selected as danger areas, to and from which flights were to be reduced. Moreover, analysis of the 1957 results suggested that in a general network for which a detailed study had not been made, a good practice would be to begin cutting on short-haul, high-density routes, if absolute numbers of overscheduled flights were to be reduced. If such a plan were followed, the least inconvenience to the flying public should result. On the other hand, viewed as a cost problem, it is evident that trimming flight assignments over long-haul routes would tend to produce the greatest cost savings per flight removed.

Further inspection of the 1957 results pointed to the fact that the extremes of overscheduling as well as excessive costs and also overpricing occurred in general on routes served by two to four competitors. Whether or not the number of competing airlines can be said to have *caused* the observed excesses, it is clear that such competition neither eliminated the tendency to overschedule nor brought the system closer to the ideal pricing patterns of a purely competitive market. The question might therefore arise whether other service improvements would be worth the price.

By comparison of route-by-route costs of overscheduling for both 1957 and 1963, it was suggested that the excesses of nonideal scheduling can be expected to become more and more costly as the present jet age continues. Measured in dollars, the economic wastes will continue to increase if scheduling continues as it has in the past.

Finally, examination of the shadow prices in the 1963 study, and their comparison with the 1957 results, showed the possibility of future price reductions along many routes and the need for increases in an extremely small number of cases. A further encouraging sign for the future of domestic air travel is that the ever-increasing demand, especially at high traffic nodes, implies larger individual "lumps" of demand over each route. Consequently, there may be a trend of increasing load factors on the jet equipment that is likely to be in operation through most of the 1960's. Thus an assumed "realistic" load factor could increase above 60 per cent. In the future the model may be closely approximated by reality. This could be the result of conscious application of analyses similar to the one presented here, either by individual airlines or by the CAB, or it could be owing to chance.

Whatever the reason, even greater price reductions would then be theoretically available to the public.

In closing, it is well to point out once again that the results presented in this chapter do not exhaust the possibilities of the linear programming models employed. Especially important is the fact that extremely efficient programs for solving very large problems on very fast machines have now become generally available. The same model could examine a larger system of nodes in finer detail, e.g., with less aircraft aggregation. It could also treat a more complex interregional system, embodying perhaps the location of maintenance facilities with differing regional labor and/or production costs. Furthermore, routines are available for parametric programming, whereby elements in either the column on the right-hand side or in the top row may be varied. In this study it would be very interesting to investigate the effects of variations in demands and also changes in cost parameters on the final allocations. As a first step, however, it is hoped that the methodology and the results of the study as presented here will prove to be of interest.

Appendices

Appendix A

Balanced Competition

BECAUSE OF THE IMPORTANCE attached by the CAB to achieving and maintaining some measure of competition, and because the policy has provoked not only much general comment but also several rather specific studies of its effectiveness, a few comments are appended here. The Board has defended much of its route award action with the argument that the provision for competitive services is required of it in the Civil Aeronautics Act and, furthermore, that duplication of carriers over a given route is a way of assuring maximum service improvements. This consideration seems to have been primary in a great many cases, to the exclusion of others. The matter has been debated heavily. The Board's position is illustrated by several statements it has made in Congressional testimony, quoted in this appendix, along with interpretations. This is followed by a few more specific comments, both pro and con, on how well the policy has worked in practice.

> Q. What weight does the Board assign to competition as a component of the public interest?
>
> A. While it is not possible to assign a quantitative value to the weight assigned to the need for competition as a component of the public interest, it is clear from Board decisions that the need for competition is a major element in such decisions. The Board has consistently regarded effective competition as a necessary and practical means of assuring the maintenance of a higher quality of service than could be achieved by complete reliance on regulatory control, and the important weight accorded the need for competition is evidenced in the fact that the Board has pursued a policy of authorizing the maximum amount of competition consistent with the sound development of the air transportation system.
>
> Q. How does the Board define effective competitition in the airline industry? What are the essential prerequisites for achieving effective

competition over particular routes, in particular regions, and in the Nation generally?

A. In terms of individual markets, effective competition may be said to exist where two or more carriers actively contend for access to available traffic on approximately even terms.

It is the Board's opinion that well-balanced route systems and financially strong carriers are the essential prerequisites for achieving effective competition over particular routes, in particular regions, and in the Nation generally.

However, it is also the Board's opinion that it is not always essential to have direct point-to-point competition to achieve this effective competition since many of the benefits of competition cannot be contained over portions of a carrier's system. For example, modern equipment purchased for competitive reasons is not restricted to use over competitive segments only, and because of the complex interrelationship between fares, lower fares produced by competitive pressure on one route or segment generally must be applied to noncompetitive segments as well.[1]

The following comments are taken from two students of government air transportation policy.

The Board has founded its policy upon . . . the belief that the existence of close competition stimulates progress in techniques of operation and service, i.e., that it brings about a more active experimentation by management in certain types of product variation and production methods than would otherwise occur. . . . For the Board, competition exists between air carriers when they are rendering services that are substitutable for each other to a significant degree.[2]

Soon after its establishment, the Board evolved a policy . . . on competition which seemed to be predicated on a stratification of the airlines into categories having common economic characteristics, with the object of maintaining "balanced competition," as opposed to undue rivalry, within each of these classifications and of gradually strengthening the smaller carriers by the addition of new routes and the extension of existing ones. Apparently the Board thought that such a policy would place the smaller airlines on a sounder basis to compete with the paralleling sections of the larger systems. . . . Presumably the Board's aim has been to allow the development of an air transport system

[1] U.S., Congress, Senate, Select Committee on Small Business, *Materials Relative to Competition in the Regulated Civil Aviation Industry, 1956*, 84th Cong., 2nd Sess., pp. 8–9.

[2] Lucille S. Keyes, *Federal Control of Entry into Air Transportation* (Cambridge: Harvard University Press, 1951), pp. 320–321.

> composed of relatively self-sufficient units, without too much difference in economic power, which are able to exist with a more or less common level of rates. This aim is, of course, a Utopian one. The history of other forms of transportation points out the difficulties of its attainment. . . . Any increase in the number of airlines complicates the attainment of anything even approaching "balanced competition." The easiest and surest path to the attainment of such a competitive situation is the reduction of the number of operators through consolidation. But, unless consolidations are forced, the likelihood of progress along that path is at best doubtful. The reason for this is that consolidations of the type most likely to occur voluntarily and most likely to result in strong new airlines — those between very large and very small carriers — have been and still seem to be those which encounter the most opposition from competitors and from the Board itself.[3]

An interesting defense of the results of the Board's general policy of competitive awards is found in the study by United Research Incorporated.[4] The essence of the argument is that, even if the Board has occasionally provided more than enough competition on a given route or set of routes, the carriers themselves are solving the problem by voluntary curtailment of service; thus service is provided only up to the limit dictated by economically sound reasoning, regardless of how much was authorized. Clearly this is not a direct defense of the Board's action, but rather takes the position that it does not matter if the Board makes mistakes in the direction of excessive authorization.

> The presumption in favor of competition provides the only reasonable assurance that the standards of service will be maintained at a high level. . . . While it is debatable whether direct competition in all instances produces the significant service gains generally claimed, it is clear that competitive markets do not suffer service-wise in comparison with noncompetitive markets;
>
> . . . .
>
> Since the review of carrier behavior in competitive markets indicates that voluntary abstention in providing service is not uncommon, it would appear that insofar as the Board errs in providing too much service in a given market, the economic penalty is not severe;
>
> . . . .

[3] John H. Frederick, *Commercial Air Transportation* (4th ed., Homewood: Richard D. Irwin, Inc., 1955), pp. 177–178.

[4] United Research Incorporated, *Federal Regulation of the Domestic Air Transport Industry* (Cambridge: United Research Incorporated, 1959).

> The observations of past experience do not show that over-authorization of competitive service has resulted either in service deterioration or substantial financial hardships. . . . [By abstention] the carriers are dealing rationally with the over-authorization problem in a way which minimizes the importance of the problem itself.[5]

The following sources indicate that there is by no means universal acceptance of the Board's policy in favor of competition. Early food for thought came in the study by Gill and Bates. Although no longer completely up to date, their results are still of interest. Important is the fact that this work has been available and widely discussed for many years, but CAB policy regarding competition has gone on undaunted.

> First, competition has been and continues to be an important force in assuring the traveler of a high standard of schedule service, especially in major markets where the ability to support the schedule patterns of the competing carrier is unquestionable even with the increased size and speed of new aircraft.
>
> Second, there is no basis for the presumption that competition will invariably bring about a higher standard of schedule service. Due consideration must be given to those factors which determine the schedule service which a particular airline can provide in a given market.
>
> Third, the fact that competition did not improve the quality of airline schedules in more than half of the markets studied is significant of the type of competitive authorizations which have accompanied the expansion of the domestic route structure. In other words, many competitive routes have been authorized over which the competing lines have not been able to improve schedule service because of the existence of other determinants of airline service which have restricted the efforts of the airline managements in these markets.
>
> Fourth, the quality of schedule service has been significantly improved in relatively few markets by the addition of a third and fourth competitor; in fact, in some cases, this amount of competition has led to a lack of significant improvements in service and even, in extreme cases, to a deterioration in service.
>
> Fifth, the only measure of schedule quality which has been improved by competition in practically all cases is that of the volume of seats scheduled or its equivalent — space availability.
>
> Sixth, the effects of striving for competitive superiority in some markets has in some instances had an adverse effect on the quality of

[5] *Ibid.*, pp. iii, 44, and 131, respectively.

schedule service which a carrier has rendered in its noncompetitive markets.[6]

And Keyes has some comments on the economic foundations of the Board's competitive policy:

> Furthermore, the Board's predilection in favor of genuinely competitive services . . . is in itself a hindrance to the achievement of optimum economic performance insofar as it results in the certification of new firms for the rendering of additional services that might be more efficiently produced by firms already serving the markets concerned. The Board's position has not been based on a contention that competition as such would insure the achievement of the economic optimum (conditional or unconditional) in the affected markets. In favoring the establishment of competition, the Board has not relied on any agreement that competition, pure or impure, must result in optimum investment or in the best possible distribution of output among firms;
>
> . . . .
>
> If air transportation is to attain a status of self-sufficiency and to carry its fair share of the cost of operating airways and airports, it must be allowed to earn a profit where this is possible unless definitely against the public interest. Multiple carrier competition has been the major flaw, as determined by this study, in the competitive expansion of the domestic air transportation system.[7]

The recent work by Meyer *et al.* indicates that the Board's policy may have had results other than price reductions for the consumer:

> Paradoxically, this limited price competition occurs more frequently in single-carrier markets than in multicarrier markets. Fear of the competitor's price reactions and his intervention on proposed rates before the CAB has apparently deterred price experimentation in multicarrier markets. Instead, competition in these markets has taken the form of rivalry in the quality of free meals, advertising, faster equipment, and other forms of service competition.[8]

In an extensive survey, Bluestone comes to very interesting conclusions regarding the advantages of the Board's policy of competitive

[6] Frederick W. Gill and Gilbert L. Bates, *Airline Competition* (Cambridge: Harvard University Printing Office, 1949), pp. 131–132.

[7] Keyes, *op. cit.*, pp. 320, 631, respectively.

[8] John Meyer, M. J. Peck, John Stenason, and Charles Zwick, *The Economics of Competition in the Transportation Industries* (Cambridge: Harvard University Press, 1959), p. 230.

route awards. After deciding that negative answers apply to the questions of whether or not competition (1) increases traffic, (2) decreases fares, or (3) improves quality, he concludes that the advantages of competition are outweighed by the costs and that competition should be drastically reduced. He further cites competition with other forms of transportation as far more important, for example, in airline fare reductions.[9]

[9] David W. Bluestone, "The Problem of Competition Among Domestic Trunk Airlines," *Journal of Air Law and Commerce*, XX (Autumn, 1953), 395.

Appendix B

Extensions of the Model

INSOFAR AS THE MODEL in the text considers less than all nodes in the domestic trunkline system, the following division is perhaps meaningful. Although the divisions may appear artificial, they indicate the sorts of complexities to be encountered in trying to cover the entire domestic air transport network. The set A may be thought of as all domestic trunk nodes considered to be within the system (i.e., included in the model); B will be the set of domestic nodes not included. Then the union of A and B, $A \cup B$, is the set of all domestic trunkline traffic nodes.

The set A may be described as containing the following elements:

a_1 those aircraft that are always within A except when called upon to help meet *unforeseen* demand in B. Unforeseen demand is defined as temporary demand within a particular set which cannot be completely satisfied by the aircraft that are normally operating in that set.

a_2 those aircraft that are always within A and between A and B (not within B), except for unforeseen demand in B.

The set B has similar elements, b_1 and b_2, with the same interpretation. Finally, there might exist common elements:

c_1 aircraft always between A and B only, except for unforeseen demand in either A or B.

c_2 aircraft always within both and between A and B

Thus if a situation of unforeseen demand were to arise in A, aircraft would be drawn from b_1, b_2, and c_1; if it arose in B, they would be drawn from a_1, a_2, and c_1.

1. "Leakage" Models: No Unforeseen Demand

Any model that considers only the movements of aircraft strictly within the bounds selected (a "nonleakage" model) would contain elements a_1 only. Such a model, however, would deny the possibility of an aircraft entering the system from outside, flying between a few nodes, and then exiting again to the outside. As will become apparent in this section, however, to allow for leakage involves either extreme simplification of the nature of the "outside" world or a great increase in the complexity of the model, and perhaps both. Essentially four possibilities exist for leakage models without any unforeseen demand:

1. All exits and entrances to A pass through a particular node a^* (such nodes will be termed "gates"); and B is considered to be concentrated at a single outside node b^o. Thus, allowance is made for entrance and exit of planes, but these movements are rigidly channeled. The part of this model that allows for leakage would include elements a_2 and c_2. Note that $a_2 \equiv c_2$ (and $c_1 \equiv b_2$), because B has been collapsed to a single point.
2. Let several (2, 3, $\cdots$, all) elements of A be gates to b^o. This model allows outmovement from several nodes within A to the single outside node, and inmovement from b^o to several inside nodes. The elements contained in the model are the same as in 1, and the same interpretation applies.
3. Let traffic into and out of A be through a^* but let it be to several (2, 3, $\cdots$, all) nodes in B. That is, B is no longer concentrated at b^o.
4. Let complete interaction between several (2, 3, $\cdots$, all) nodes in both A and B be possible.

Models 3 and 4 may be treated together. Both imply extensive knowledge about the nodes in B and also the inclusion of the gate nodes of B in the model. If this is possible, then it is difficult to see why the gates in B (and, in the limit, the entire set $A \cup B$) were not treated as a complete unit from the beginning. Presumably the object in having the set A contain less than the total universe is because it is operationally infeasible to treat the entire system directly, either owing to problems of size or because of lack of adequate knowledge about all nodes. It may be concluded that only models that incorporate leakage to and from a *point* are feasible; viz., models of type 1 or 2.

The model presented on pp. 59 and 60 could be expanded along the lines suggested in Models 1 and 2. In the former case, it would be necessary to add the following elements (where superscripts * and ^{o} indicate the single gate in A and the only point in B, respectively):

To the objective function add

$$\sum_h \sum_r {}^*_r c^o_h \, {}^*_r x^o_h + \sum_h \sum_r {}^o_r c^*_h \, {}^o_r x^*_h$$

Alter the constraints as follows:

1. $${}^*y^{oo} = {}^*D^o$$
$${}^oy^{**} = {}^oD^*$$
$$\left.\begin{aligned} {}^Jy^{*o} &= {}^JD^o \\ {}^oy^{*L} &= {}^oD^L \end{aligned}\right\} \text{ for each node in } A \text{ except the gate } a^*$$

2. $$\sum_r {}^o_r x^*_h - \sum_r {}^*_r x^o_h \geq 0$$

3. Add $-\sum_r {}^*_r b^o_h \, {}^*_r x^o_h - \sum_r {}^o_r b^*_h \, {}^o_r x^*_h$ to the left-hand side of 3 in the original model

4. $$\sum_h \sum_r {}^*_r a^o_h \, {}^*_r x^o_h - {}^*y^{oo} \geq 0$$
$$\sum_h \sum_r {}^o_r a^*_h \, {}^o_r x^*_h - \sum_L {}^oy^{*L} \geq 0$$ (where L takes on the value * along with all others)

For the case indicated in Model 2, the adjustment is even simpler. Merely allow all superscripts J, K, and L, to take on the value o as well as all former values; i.e., they can be used as designations for the single node outside of A. This applies both to the objective function and also to the constraints.

2. Unforeseen Demand Models

By definition, unforeseen demand models will be ones that include leakage. Thus all modifications for unforeseen demand would be added to an original model that already contained revisions for Models 1 or 2 as before.

To begin with the simplest case, assume the following: first, all B at b^o; second, all movement to and from A through gate a^*; third, no unforeseen demand in B (i.e., at b^o). The following possibilities for unforeseen demand would still exist:

i. At a^*
   1. To b^o
   2. To another node a^J
   3. To b^o and a single a^J
   4. To several (or all) other a^J
   5. To b^o and several (all) other a^J

ii. At a^J
   1. To another a^K (may be a^*)
   2. To several (all) a^K
   3. To b (via a^*). This is a combination of ii.1 (with a^*) and i.1.

iii. At several (all) a^J
   1. To another a^K (may be a^*)
   2. To several (all) a^K
   3. To b (via a^*). This is a combination, of iii.1 (with a^*) and i.1.

The general procedure for handling such cases will be sketched for two examples only:

i.1 *a^* to b^o*. The objective function would include another new term:

$$+ \sum_h {}^o_0c^*_h \; {}^o_0x^*_h$$

where the $r = 0$ subscript indicates an empty flight, i.e., the ferrying of an aircraft to meet the unforeseen demands. Note that r may not take on the value 0 in the other terms of the objective function, since the definition of unforeseen demand precludes the possibility of an aircraft coming from *within* the system.

The following notation is necessary:

ρ = amount of unforeseen demand
V = maximum carrying capacity } for a given type of aircraft over a given route
μ = "break-even" capacity } for a given type of aircraft over a given route
p = ticket price (revenue)

Presumably, the decision whether or not the unanticipated demand can be satisfied rests first, on having the aircraft available after the total demands in the system, as expressed by D's, have been met; and second, on cost considerations. From the viewpoint of the individual airline, the need for a balance of costs and anticipated revenues is clear. This behavior could be extended to a regulatory body as well, thereby emphasizing the basically secondary nature of anticipated demand. An additional constraint set would be necessary:

$$ {}^{o}_{0}c^{*}_{h} < {}^{*}p^{o}\,{}^{*}V^{o}_{h} - {}^{*}_{V}c^{o}_{h} \quad \text{if} \quad {}^{*}\rho^{o} \geq {}^{*}V^{o}_{h} $$
$$ {}^{o}_{0}c^{*}_{h} < {}^{*}p^{o}\,{}^{*}\rho^{o} - {}^{*}_{\rho}c^{o}_{h} \quad \text{if} \quad {}^{*}\mu^{o} \leq {}^{*}\rho^{o} < {}^{*}V^{o}_{h} $$

If ${}^{*}\rho^{o} < {}^{*}\mu^{o}$, the demand would not be met.

ii.1 *a^J to another a^K.* The addition to the objective function would be the same as in the model immediately preceding. The new constraint set would now read (where ${}^{*}c^{J}$ = cost of flying a particular type of equipment from a^* to a^J):

$$ {}^{o}_{0}c^{*}_{h} + {}^{*}_{0}c^{J}_{h} < {}^{J}p^{K}\,{}^{J}V^{K}_{h} - {}^{J}_{V}c^{K}_{h} \quad \text{if} \quad {}^{J}\rho^{K} \geq {}^{J}V^{K}_{h} $$
$$ {}^{o}_{0}c^{*}_{h} + {}^{*}_{0}c^{J}_{h} < {}^{J}p^{K}\,{}^{J}\rho^{K} - {}^{J}_{\rho}c^{K}_{h} \quad \text{if} \quad {}^{*}\mu^{JK} \leq {}^{J}\rho^{K} < {}^{J}V^{K}_{h} $$

And no service would be offered if ${}^{J}\rho^{K} < {}^{*}\mu^{JK}$. Furthermore, this modification should also consider the cost of moving the "outside" aircraft back to b^o (via a^*), without passengers, after completion of the mission.

After exhausting a list of possibilities with modifications similar to to those just suggested, one would have to expand the gates in A to several and finally all a^J in order to approach realism. Set B would remain concentrated at the unique node b^o. Clearly, this becomes prohibitively large.

There is, however, a general case that can be made against the use of unforeseen demand models. It rests on the fact that most airlines keep "spares" at particular traffic nodes throughout the network. These are aircraft whose function it is to be available if unforeseen circumstances should arise (e.g., arrivals delayed by weather, accidents, equipment malfunctions, irregular delays in maintenance, excessive demand, etc.). Thus they are designed to meet the very demand contingencies that have been already discussed. Let the second subscript s denote spares; then one could add to the objective function a term $\sum_{J}\sum_{h} {}^{J}c_{hs}\,{}^{J}x_{hs}$, where the ${}^{J}c_{hs}$ is a storage cost for airplane type h at node J. Since airlines seem to plan in terms of a minimal percentage ϕ of their total fleet that must be available as spares at any given time,[1] one could include a constraint of the sort $\sum_{J}\sum_{h} {}^{J}x_{hs} \geq \phi S_T$

[1] Cf. Joseph L. Nicholson, *Air Transport Management* (New York: John Wiley & Sons, Inc., 1951), p. 322, where experience of one large airline suggested 8 per cent as a value for ϕ.

(where S_T = total airplane fleet). Obviously, however, the item in the objective function is minimized when equality holds in the constraint. Since S_T and ϕ are known quantities, the entire unforeseen demand problem, insofar as it is solved by the use of spares, can be treated by decreasing the total available fleet size by an appropriate amount. This means a downward adjustment of actual values of the S_h in the availability constraints.

3. Maintenance

No mention was made of the fact that, in the course of operating within a given time period, aircraft require maintenance. Essentially three types of maintenance exist.[2]

1. Line maintenance — all work performed on the aircraft without removing it from service. It is done between flights at all nodes.
2. Overhaul — all work necessitating removal of the aircraft from service. It is accomplished on a periodic basis at particular maintenance facilities only.
3. Repair — unscheduled maintenance necessary because of unexpected damage or malfunction.

It will be assumed that line maintenance occurs at each node between flights as required and is reflected in the number of hours which a given aircraft is available for flight assignment during any time period. Repair is necessary irregularly, by definition, and it is partly for this reason that spares exist at certain key points within an air transportation network. However, overhaul deserves further consideration. It may be performed:

a. At one node within the system.
b. At several such nodes.
c. At one outside point.
d. At several outside points.[3]

[2] See R. Dixon Speas, *Technical Aspects of Air Transport Management* (New York: McGraw-Hill Book Company, Inc., 1955), pp. 158–159.

[3] However, *a* seems by far the most prevalent, at least among the domestic trunklines. United States trunklines have the following "major overhaul" facilities: American Airlines — New York and Tulsa; Trans World Airlines — New York and Kansas City; Northeast Airlines — Boston; Northwest Airlines — Minneapolis; National Airlines — Jacksonville; Eastern Air Lines — Miami; Delta Air Lines — Atlanta; Continental Air Lines — Denver; Western Air Lines — Burbank; Braniff Airways — Dallas; Capital Airlines — Washington, D. C.; United Air Lines — San Francisco. From George P. Baker and Gayton E. Germane, *Case Problems in Transportation Management* (New York: McGraw-Hill Book Company, Inc., 1957), p. 92.

For situation *c*, one could add the following terms to the objective function: $\sum_J\sum_h {}^J_0c^M_h\,{}^J_0x^M_h + \sum_J\sum_h {}^M_0c^J_h\,{}^M_0x^J_h$, where the superscript M indicates the (outside) maintenance point, to and from which aircraft would fly without passengers. This is a type of leakage, and passage between the system and the maintenance facility could either be through a single gate a^* or through several (2, 3, · · · , all) nodes. Thus in $\sum_J\sum_h {}^J_0c^M_h\,{}^J_0x^M_h$, J either takes on the value * only, or, in the latter case, several or all values within the system. Most probably only a small number of nodes would act as gates, since planes would logically be scheduled to carry passengers to one of the near-maintenance nodes rather than to fly empty from a distant node to the maintenance facility.

In the constraints it would be necessary to include a checking device such that, after each flight, each individual aircraft is "cleared" for the next proposed flight. Since overhaul occurs periodically, assume every H hours, then before each planned flight of each particular airplane, the logged hours to that point must be compared with H. If they are less than H, the hours to be used on the forthcoming flight plus those necessary to reach the maintenance facility must be added to the logged total. If this still is less than H, the next flight may proceed. If not, another (shorter) use must be found for the airplane in question, or it may be sent immediately to overhaul.

Note that, in considering situation *d*, a new choice may enter. This model would include all of the above refinements plus the fact that the superscript M takes on several values, indicating several possible outside points for maintenance. Then the possibility of distributing aircraft among bases becomes important, e.g., the cost of waiting (queueing), if that is necessary, at a nearby facility must be balanced against the cost involved in flying empty to a more distant facility that is not currently occupied or is less full.

Situations *a* and *b* would incorporate all that has been said about *c* and *d*, with the further modification that r need not be zero; i.e., passengers may be carried en route to maintenance.

This brief sketch has served to show the particular complexity of optimally scheduling overhaul for each individual aircraft in the entire system under control. In fact, problems of this sort are frequently treated in and of themselves, not merely as additional clauses on a structure that is primarily addressed to a somewhat different set of questions.[4] There is, however, a convincing reason for the inapplicability of the preceding formulations in the model that is of interest in this study. These formulations would be reasonable only in the case of a single airline which had its own maintenance base (or a group of airlines if they used the same maintenance facilities). For a problem wherein the equipment of various airlines is to be aggregated in order to answer questions concerning the total numbers of flights over several routes served by several airlines, the concept of one or several overhaul bases to which this generalized equipment (i.e., equipment without a particular airline identity) should be channeled is of little real value.

Yet maintenance does occur and must be recognized. For this reason an assumption will be introduced. All overhaul will be assumed to be (1) carried out at particular traffic nodes within the system, and (2) accomplished on a staggered basis. This may be either the "continuous" or the "block" type. The former, as practiced by Eastern Air Lines at Miami, divides and subdivides periodic maintenance programs to cover specific overhaul items on a staggered basis. The latter, used by Delta Air Lines in Atlanta, consists of an eight-way breakdown of the normal major overhaul cycle to deal with a specific area of an airframe at any one time.[5]

This study recognizes that all types of maintenance have an effect on the number of hours for which any aircraft is available during a period of time. Both line maintenance and overhaul will be treated by reducing the total available hours appropriately (see p. 79). Since repair is necessary only in unforeseen cases, it will not be treated explicitly. This is one of the reasons for the existence of spares.

[4] See, for example, T. E. Bartlett and A. Charnes, "Cyclic Scheduling and Combinatorial Topology: Assignment and Routing of Motive Power to Meet Scheduling and Maintenance Requirements. Part II — Generalization and Analysis," *Naval Research Logistics Quarterly*, IV (September, 1957), 207–220; also Baker and Germane, *op. cit.*, pp. 84–90, 470.

[5] See *Aviation Week*, March 30, 1959, p. 45: "In this way, no airplane is held in company hangars for more than five days at one time, a significant advantage when compared with the twenty or thirty days aircraft would be tied up for major overhaul under the old system of complete maintenance every 16,000 hours." In addition, the discussion in Baker and Germane, *op. cit.*, pp. 84–93, makes clear the fact that the locations of maintenance bases have been considered in terms of the existing route structure and accompanying flight schedules and thus were designed to be available in an efficient manner to equipment during its normal utilization scheduling.

Appendix C

Airline Demand Forecasting

MUCH INTEREST has been shown in the motivation behind air travel. Studies concerned with the current status of airline demand or its probable magnitude in the very near future usually employ simple indices reflecting the general national economic climate. For longer-range forecasts, or for questions of developing new potential demand areas, other factors, often of a more sociological nature, are included.

Since passenger forecasts for the near future are necessary in this study, a brief outline of some of the recent discussions will not be out of place. The material that follows is arranged according to type of institution responsible for the work.

1. Airlines

It is of interest to note that forecasting is an extremely important element in the commercial air transportation industry. Every domestic trunk airline currently prepares forecasts of passenger revenue.[1] Trunklines have cited the following factors as relevant in the preparation of a forecast:[2]

Past company and industry growth.
General economic activity.
Type and capacity of aircraft and equipment available.
Judgment of company executives.

[1] Jack B. Jarvis, *Passenger Mile and Revenue Forecasting Practices* (Renton, Washington: Boeing Airplane Company, Transport Division, 1958), p. 13. This appendix draws on this source and also on L. C. Hansen *Mathematics and Forecasting: The Prediction of Air Traffic* (Renton, Washington: Boeing Airplane Company, Transport Division, 1958.)

[2] Jarvis, *op. cit.*, pp. 14–15. The information comes from a questionnaire, to which the following trunklines responded: American, Capital, Continental, Delta, Eastern, National, Northeast, Trans World, United, Western.

Action of competitors.

Seasonal variations.

Probable effects of CAB decisions upon existing competition.

These are weighted in various ways, depending on whether the forecast is for a short-period, annual, or longer-range purpose.

The primary methods used by airlines appear to be

a. Trend and cycle analysis. Historic sales records are analyzed in an effort to discover long-term growth trends, cyclical fluctuations seasonal variations, and random fluctuations. This is standard time series analysis, and it is applied by the airlines with varying degrees of sophistication.

b. Judgment of company executives. Very widely cited, this is frequently based on wide experience and study of transportation, social, and general economic conditions; but by definition it differs among companies.[3]

c. Correlation analysis. The following pairs are frequently used: GNP and intercity common carrier traffic, total air traffic, and company passenger volume. This method seems less widely used, however, than the preceding two.

The Boeing studies suggest that, as one might expect, shorter-run forecasts tend generally to be reasonably accurate, whereas the longer ones are not. Table C-1 provides comparisons.

2. Government and Manufacturers

After examination of existing forecasts, it becomes apparent that government, trade, and manufacturing organizations also put forth a great deal of time and effort in formulating estimates of domestic air passenger traffic. It is therefore of interest to look briefly at their methods and results.

Aircraft companies have generally found that trends in the national economy and the behavior of airline passenger-miles could be mathematically related. Government, trade, and manufacturing organizations cite the following as currently in use:[4]

Linear or curvilinear projections of historic trends.

Simple or multiple correlation analysis.

[3] A vice-president of a major airline has been quoted as follows: "In the end, the forecast is based largely upon executive judgment and experience. Mechanical forecasts and formulas are not useful in this field," Jarvis, *op. cit.*, p. 57.

[4] *Ibid.*, pp. 56–57.

TABLE C-1. TRUNKLINE FORECASTS OF DOMESTIC SCHEDULED PASSENGER-MILE TRAFFIC (SHORTER-RANGE FORECASTS)

(Billions of Miles)

	1958			1959			Forecasts[a]		
Airline	Actual	Forecast[a]	Per Cent Deviation[b]	Actual	Forecast[a]	Per Cent Deviation[b]	1960	1961	1962
American	4.891	5.503	+12.5[c]	5.388	6.204	+15.1[d]	6.729	7.562	8.039
Braniff	0.931	0.923	−0.9	0.946	1.075	+13.6	1.186	1.314	1.445
Capital	1.413	1.678	+18.8[c]	1.638	1.619	−1.2	1.498	2.019	2.265
Continental	0.419	0.479	+14.3	0.642	0.633	−1.4	0.733	0.761	0.816
Delta	1.400	1.511	+7.9	1.570	1.740	+10.8	2.002	2.325	2.628
Eastern	3.811	4.732	+24.2[c]	4.051	5.371	+7.9[d]	6.669	6.710	7.247
National	0.900	1.337	+35.1	1.141	1.420	−1.8	1.937	2.880	2.880
Northeast	0.407	0.537	+31.9	0.536	0.856	+59.7	0.872	1.297	1.329
Northwest	1.111	1.082	−2.6	1.379	1.260	−8.6	1.400	1.532	1.656
Trans World	3.662	3.933	+7.4[c]	4.468	4.682	+4.8	5.145	5.557	5.968
United	4.915	4.935	+0.4	4.906	5.181	+5.6	5.930	6.555	7.112
Western	0.503	0.802	+59.4[c]	0.875	0.985	+12.6	1.104	1.238	1.358
Totals	24.435	27.450		27.540	31.026		35.225	39.750	42.743

a. Forecasts were prepared in 1957 and early 1958.
b. Per cent deviation = [(Forecast − Actual)/(Actual)](100).
c. Strikes of the following duration occurred during 1958: American — 12 days; Capital — 38 days; Eastern — 38 days; Trans World — 18 days; Western — 109 days.
d. Strikes during 1959 (continuations of ones begun in 1958): American — 11 days; Eastern — 2 days. Civil Aeronautics Board, *Monthly Report of Air Carrier Traffic Statistics*, November, 1959, p. 51.

Sources: 1959 Actual figures from Civil Aeronautics Board, *Monthly Report of Air Carrier Traffic Statistics*, November, 1959, pp. 25, 29–31. All other traffic figures from Jarvis, *op. cit.*, p. 28.

Executive judgment.
Economic models.
Statistical and mathematical formulas.
Marketing surveys.

Early techniques, beginning in 1944, frequently used an index of economic growth and the "national economy penetration factor" approach whereby (1) the total transportation industry was assumed to grow at the same rate as the national economy, and (2) each transportation mode was analyzed separately (with regard to its so-called competitive penetration capabilities) and allocated a share of the total transportation market.[5] Two underlying assumptions that characterized these early forecasts have subsequently been modified. They were first, that the national economy grows at a relatively slow rate, and second, that the private automobile would dominate the total transportation market to the detriment of the common carriers, especially airlines. The Curtiss-Wright forecasts were occasionally quite satisfactory, but, again, the longer-range attempts were not particularly good. Table C-2 shows these results.

By 1956, a change in underlying assumptions in many of the forecasts was evident, although the methods employed were basically the same.[6] Increasing appearance of wider-range estimates is noticeable; i.e., forecasts include high, low, and expected estimates of traffic. The growth of the economy is more frequently discussed as "vigorous"

[5] The following forecasts, by virtue of basic philosophy and date of publication (1944–1954), are grouped in this early category: B. A. McDonald and J. L. Drew, "Air Transportation in the Immediate Postwar Period," Report No. BR-69, Curtiss-Wright Corporation, Airplane Division, Business Research Department, March, 1944, NA. (The designation NA will be attached to those studies which were not available to the present writer, who is therefore indebted to the discussion of them in the Boeing publications mentioned in footnote 1.) Also included are G. H. Aldrich, "Airline Passenger Market — The Next 10 Years," *Aviation Age*, March, 1954, pp. 28–45, and several early analyses by the Port of New York Authority.

[6] This more recent period will include the following reports: U.S., Civil Aeronautics Administration, *1960–1965–1970 Civil Aviation and Federal Airways Forecasts* (Washington, D. C.: U.S. Department of Commerce, 1956); K. H. Larrson, "A Critical Review of Earlier Forecasts of Air Traffic and a New Approach" (Montreal: Canadair Ltd., Sales Engineering Division, 1956) (NA); Boeing Airplane Company, *Traffic Forecast of Domestic United States Airlines to 1965* (Renton, Washington: Boeing Airplane Company, Transport Division, 1956); Boeing Airplane Company, *Forecast of Free World Passenger and Cargo Air Traffic (1965–1970–1975)* (Renton, Washington: Boeing Airplane Company, Transport Division, 1959); "U.S. Domestic Trunkline Traffic Development and Forecasts Through 1970," *Report SE No. 259–1* (San Diego: Convair Corporation, 1957); Port of New York Authority, *Forecasts of the United States Domestic Air Passenger Market, 1965–1975* (New York: Port of New York Authority, 1957).

TABLE C-2. EARLY FORECASTS
(Billions of Passenger-Miles)

		Forecasts								
				Port of New York Authority						
Year	Actual	Curtiss-Wright	Per Cent Deviation	1944	Per Cent Deviation	1950[a]	Per Cent Deviation	*Aviation Age*[a] (1954)	Per Cent Deviation
1946	5.9	4.7	−20.3	—	—	—	—	—	—
1947	6.1	5.5	−9.8	—	—	—	—	—	—
1948	5.9	6.1	+3.4	—	—	—	—	—	—
1949	6.7	6.6	−1.5	—	—	—	—	—	—
1950	8.0	7.0	−12.5	9.5	+18.8	6.6	−17.5	—	—
1955	19.7	—	—	30.0	+52.3	11.1	−43.7	17.3	−12.2

a. Both of these forecasts extend beyond 1955, and they will also be included later in Table C-3.

Source: Forecast figures from Jarvis, *op. cit., passim.* It is well to point out here, however, that with one exception (out of a total of ten) the figures given as "Per cent of Deviation" in this reference are incorrect. The Per Cent Deviations shown here and used throughout this study are [(Forecast − Actual)/(Actual)](100).

rather than simply "steady." Furthermore, it is more generally assumed that an ever-increasing share of the total transportation market will be handled by aviation; i.e., airline traffic is projected as an increasing rather than constant share of future total traffic.[7] Factors included for analysis also increased in some cases, as indicated by Boeing Airplane Company's consideration of historical and probable future trends of twenty-seven statistics.[8] New methods were also introduced. For instance, Canadair abstracted the air passenger industry from all other transportation industries, and remarkably accurate predictions were made on the basis of historic growth and marketing factors that enter into the public acceptance of air transportation; general economic activity was not considered.

Another technique has been adopted by the Port of New York Authority.[9] The foundations for this study are to be found in a detailed marketing survey. This is a more sociological approach, insofar as it investigates the nature of the basic market and the varying effects of consumer attitudes and habits upon travel.[10] Air travel is treated as one commodity in competition with others for a part of the buyer's dollar. The results are in terms of the ultimate consumers, i.e., passenger traffic, not passenger-miles. The performance of some of these forecasts is shown in Table C-3.

3. Independent Studies

In addition to those forecasts made by industry and government, there are a number of independent studies. Most of these have been

[7] The importance of economic trends and the growing importance of air travel are taken into consideration in a study that represents essentially the aircraft industry approach. See L. B. Aschenbeck, "Passenger Airline Economics," *Aeronautical Engineering Review*, XV (December, 1956), 39–43. The author is associated with Douglas Aircraft Company, Inc. A similar study, which is quite detailed and uses the same techniques of GNP projection and increasing penetration by air carriers of the total common carrier market, is Aeronautical Research Foundation, *National Requirements for Aviation Facilities, 1956–75*, Volume IV, "Forecast of Aviation Activity" (Washington, D. C.: U.S. Government Printing Office, 1957). An extensive survey that included air travel is L. J. Paradiso and C. Wilson, "Consumer Expenditure–Income Patterns," *Survey of Current Business*, XXXV (September, 1955), 25–32. Variations in expenditure on air travel for changes in disposable personal income are quantified. The results are also discussed in Aschenbeck, *op. cit.*

[8] This appears in the 1956 Boeing forecasts.

[9] Port of New York Authority, 1957 forecasts, *op. cit.*

[10] Its originators feel strongly about previous work: "Experience has indicated, however, that rates of air traffic growth cannot be adequately explained or projected by the theories and methods that have heretofore been generally accepted and reflected in earlier forecasts," *ibid.*, p. 18.

TABLE C-3. LONGER-RANGE FORECASTS

(Billions of Passenger-Miles)

Year	Port of New York Authority (1950)	*Aviation Age* (1954)	Canadair (1956)	Boeing (1956)	Boeing (1959)	Convair (1957)	CAA (1956)	Actual Traffic
1955	11.1 (−43.7)	17.3 (−12.2)	19.2 (−2.5)					19.7
1956			21.7 (−2.7)	22.5 (+0.9)		21.1 (−4.9)	22.4 (+0.4)	22.3
1957			24.6 (−2.8)	26.0 (+2.8)		24.8 (−2.0)		25.3
1958			27.6 (+9.1)	29.2 (+15.4)		27.2 (+7.5)		25.3
1959			30.8 (+5.5)	35.1 (+20.2)		29.7 (+1.7)		29.2
1960	14.3 (−53.0)	21.1 (−30.6)	34.1 (+12.2)	46.0 (+51.3)		32.7 (+7.6)	35.0 (+15.1)	30.4
1961			37.6	58.0		36.6		
1962			41.2	70.0		40.6		
1963			45.0	80.0		43.9		
1964			48.9	86.0		47.4		
1965	16.7	24.8	52.8	90.0	60.4	50.7	49.0	
1966			56.9			53.5		
1967			61.0			56.7		
1968			65.2			60.0		
1969			69.5			62.8		
1970	19.3	27.8	73.8		88.8	65.4	60.0	
1975	21.5				129.7			
1980	22.3							

N.B. Figures in parentheses inside the table are percentage deviations; i.e., [(Forecast − Actual)/(Actual)](100).

Sources: Figures prior to 1959 from Jarvis, *op. cit.*, p. 53.
Boeing 1959 figures from Boeing Airplane Company, *Forecast of Free World Passenger and Cargo Air Traffic*, *op. cit.*, p. 7.

written by students of economic, sociological, or psychological motivations involved in travel in general. Some deal specifically with air travel. Not all of them produce numerical results; they may be concerned with the underlying theory exclusively. Of most interest is the extensive literature that exists on gravity and spatial interaction models.[11] In general terms, these formulations deal with probable or expected numbers of trips (termed interactions) between regions or areas. Taking inspiration from the field of physics, the number of interactions is represented as varying directly with the product of masses and inversely with intervening distance. Measurement of mass is usually in terms of regional populations, although for particular studies such items as dollar volumes of trade, regional income, or employment, for example, may be more appropriate. Likewise, the distance variable need not be in terms of miles separating the regions under study; transportation cost, travel time, or fuel consumption for a specific mode of transport may be more relevant in some cases.

The work of the Civil Aeronautics Administration in this area is largely the result of investigations by D'Arcy Harvey of that organization.[12] The development and employment of P_1P_2/D seems to be presented as original; at least no reference is made to prior studies. There is, furthermore, no doubt about the role of D: "The number of airline passengers, other things being equal, will vary inversely with the distance between the communities."[13] However, certain secondary factors are mentioned as demanding attention as well.[14] The Mayhill article criticizes some of the presentations and suggests that, in view of the wide use to which these measures are put within the planning

[11] See W. Isard, *Methods of Regional Analysis: an Introduction to Regional Science* (New York: The Technology Press of M.I.T. and John Wiley & Sons, Inc., 1960), pp. 493–512, for a thorough treatment of the basic model types. The bibliography there cited covers the important historical developments as well as applications.

[12] See D'Arcy Harvey, "Airline Passenger Traffic Pattern Within the United States," *Journal of Air Law and Commerce*, XVIII (Spring, 1951), 157–165; Frederick B. Lee, "How CAA Forecasts Air Traffic Potential," *SAE Journal*, LIX (April, 1951), 44–45; D. Harvey, "Air Traffic Facts," *Aeronautical Engineering Review*, XV (July, 1956), 58–61; also G. Roger Mayhill, "A Critique of the CAA Studies on Air Traffic Generation in the United States," *Journal of Air Law and Commerce*, XX (Spring, 1953), 158–177.

[13] Harvey, *Journal of Air Law and Commerce*, *op. cit.*, p. 158.

[14] These are (1) differences in the air/surface density ratio (not defined), (2) minimum effective distance for present-day aircraft, (3) economic character of each community in a pair, (4) density of communities within a geographic area. See Harvey, *Aeronautical Engineering Review*, *op. cit.*, p. 59.

departments of the government air regulatory agencies, the logic and exposition should be made more clear and rigorous. He also suggests that the P_1P_2/D formulation may be useful chiefly as an indication of *potential* traffic.[15]

Two articles by Samuel Richmond are of interest.[16] The first deals with predicting traffic between two points under one of the special conditions that (1) new airline service is instituted between the points, or (2) if some airline service already exists, the quality of that service is changed. Data for 1952 traffic in and out of Denver provide the bases for an equation in which the number of hotel registrants in Denver from the community in question turns out to be an important datum. The second article also points out the usefulness of hotel registrants as a measure of "community of interest" between two cities, but more importantly it concludes that there is no inverse relation between number of trips and distance: "The relation in the short distances seems to be some sort of direct function and, beyond the critical distance, there is no relation at all [with distance]."[17] This is clear contradiction of the P_1P_2/D hypothesis, at least for air travel.

Further conclusions casting doubt on the importance of the distance factor have been published by Daniel Belmont in several places.[18]

He presents equations fitted by the method of least squares to data for September 17–30, 1955. They are of two types — with and without distance explicitly considered. Parameters for both types are fitted for long-distance (over 800 miles), medium-distance (400–800 miles),

[15] Testimony of Joseph Blatt, Assistant Administrator of Civil Aeronautics for Planning Research and Development, suggests that the potential nature of the index is not always kept in mind. See U.S., Congress, House, Subcommittee of the Committee on Government Operations, *Hearings, Federal Role in Aviation*, 84th Cong., 2d Sess., 1956, p. 288.

[16] Samuel B. Richmond, "Forecasting Air Passenger Traffic by Multiple Regression Analysis," *Journal of Air Law and Commerce*, XXII (Autumn, 1955), 437–444, and "Interspacial Relationships Affecting Air Travel," *Land Economics*, XXXIII (February, 1957), 65–73.

[17] Richmond, *Land Economics*, *op. cit.*, p. 73. The minimum (critical) intervening distance appears to be between 120 and 200 miles, before which air travel does not "come into its own" and beyond which the influence of distance is nil. See *ibid.*, pp. 66, 72.

[18] Daniel M. Belmont, "A Pattern of Interstation Airline Traffic," *Proceedings of the American Society of Civil Engineers*, LXXXII (May, 1956), 987-1–987-16; "A Study of Airline Interstation Traffic," *Journal of Air Law and Commerce*, XXV (Summer, 1958), 361–368; and the complete report "A Study of Airline Interstation Traffic," Research Report No. 26, The Institute of Transportation and Traffic Engineering, University of California, January, 1958.

and all routes combined. The results are compared in an F-test for significance of the difference between the two equation types. On the basis of the published figures, his conclusions are valid.[19]

Testing for improvement in the correlation index when the equation containing distance was used led to the following results: (*a*) for long-distance routes the improvement was not significant at the 5 per cent level; (*b*) for medium-distance routes the improvement was significant at the 5 per cent level; (*c*) for combined routes (the total sample) the improvement was not significant at the $\frac{1}{2}$ per cent level.[20]

In the present study, Belmont's techniques were carried out for routes being considered in 1963. This was done for comparative purposes. The steps involved several assumptions:

1. The CAA forecast of 82.2 million passengers in 1963 was used as a base.

2. As cited in the main projections in the body of this study, the findings of relatively constant percentages in particular cities were employed. The figure 82.2 million was thus multiplied by these percentages to get total traffic at each city. This yearly figure was divided by 26 to put it on a two-week basis compatible with the Belmont formulation.[21]

3. These total traffic figures were used, along with interstation air distance, in his combined formula:

$$T_{ij} = k(T_iT_j)^p/D^q$$

which is fitted as

$$\log T_{ij} = -\ 6.90755 + 1.164780 \log (T_iT_j) - 0.40950 \log D$$

where T_{ij} is total traffic (both directions) between i and j and T_iT_j represents total passengers originating and terminating at i and at j.

4. This figure is halved (to reduce it from a two-week to a one-week period) and compared with the sum of D_{ij} and D_{ji} as found by the trend prediction method employed for the projections in this study. The results are shown in Table C-4.

[19] Belmont does not regard his work as final but rather as indicating an area for more extensive research. Several routes were excluded from consideration because they did not seem to be "normal"; e.g., much Florida traffic, as well as Philadelphia originations (this latter being "overshadowed" by New York City), was excluded.

[20] Belmont, Research Report No. 26, *op. cit.*, p. 9.

[21] The fact that the Belmont equations apply only to data that have been "normalized" in this particular way is not emphasized in the report.

TABLE C-4. 1963 WEEKLY TRAFFIC FORECAST COMPARISONS

(Both Directions)

Route		Trend Prediction Method (See Chapter 5, Section 2)	Belmont Method
Boston	– Chicago	5,210	4,730
	– Cleveland	1,840	950
	– Detroit	1,610	1,290
	– Los Angeles	3,210	1,610
	– Miami	6,490	1,130
	– New York	31,940	11,750
	– San Francisco	1,660	980
	– Washington	7,095	2,820
Chicago	– Cleveland	5,265	5,550
	– Detroit	7,230	9,125
	– Los Angeles	8,060	8,000
	– Miami	11,120	5,310
	– New York	32,560	30,600
	– San Francisco	2,820	5,350
	– Washington	5,460	10,900
Cleveland	– Detroit	2,080	2,085
	– Los Angeles	2,220	1,265
	– Miami	5,230	930
	– New York	12,540	6,480
	– San Francisco	660	850
	– Washington	2,245	2,410
Detroit	– Los Angeles	2,455	1,840
	– Miami	6,190	1,285
	– New York	11,800	8,525
	– San Francisco	870	1,240
	– Washington	2,380	3,060
Los Angeles	– Miami	1,415	1,915
	– New York	17,110	9,170
	– San Francisco	29,700	5,320
	– Washington	4,440	3,100
Miami	– New York	33,385	7,240
	– San Francisco	600	1,225
	– Washington	3,890	2,565
New York	– San Francisco	9,350	6,180
	– Washington	26,040	21,900
San Francisco	– Washington	3,700	2,060

It is clear that the two methods rest on differing assumptions. Insofar as projections made by the use of the Belmont formula depend on intercity air distances (which are constant) and on a pair of total traffic figures for various centers (which is a particular constant percentage, for a given city, of total expected domestic traffic), it is apparent that in fact a *constant* per cent of total domestic traffic on each given route is implied. In effect, a line of zero slope is projected (where the coordinate axes measure time and per cent of total national traffic on a given route). The y-intercept is not the mean value over a period of years, but rather a figure derived from the sample period September 17–30, 1955. This is a fundamental difference from the least-squares lines used in the body of this study, and Table C-4 is presented to facilitate comparison of the two methods with actual traffic occurring in 1963.

The works of Richmond and Belmont, while not always in agreement regarding the precise role played by distance,[22] cast some doubt on heretofore accepted theory.

Several publications from the Survey Research Center at the University of Michigan concern themselves with air travel.[23] Chief interest is focused on expressing purchases of air trips (and especially nonbusiness travel) as a function of several variables such as experience in flying, rail travel, income, occupation, distance from airport, and fare. The last of these references lists business executives as the most frequent users of air transportation. In using the proportion of families

[22] Hansen, *op. cit.*, p. 27, gives the misleading impression that Belmont's work is simply an elaboration and quantification of Richmond's.

[23] John B. Lansing, *The Place of Air Travel in the Travel Market* (Ann Arbor: University of Michigan, 1956) (mimeographed); John B. Lansing and Ernest Lilienstein, *The Travel Market, 1955*, a report to the Travel Research Association (Ann Arbor: University of Michigan, 1957); John B. Lansing and Dwight M. Blood, "A Cross-Section Analysis of Non-Business Air Travel" (abstract), *Econometrica*, XXVI (April, 1958), 315–316; and John B. Lansing, Jung-Chao Liu, and Daniel B. Suits, "An Analysis of Interurban Air Travel," *Quarterly Journal of Economics*, LXXV (February, 1961), 87–95. On a smaller scale, a study has been made of factors involved in the use of the airplane as a mode of travel in the Detroit metropolitan area. See Basil Zimmer, "Factors Related to Air Travel in a Large Metropolitan Center," *Land Economics*, XXXV (February, 1959), 67–71, where it is concluded that air transportation is used predominantly by males and for business trips (70). This statement on the role of business travel is in contrast to many other estimates of the relative roles of business and pleasure travel. See pp. 75–77 of present volume. T. P. Wright, "Economic Factors in Air Transportation," *Aeronautical Engineering Review*, XVI (April, 1957), 45–61, offers a curious approach. The "inverse-cube" relationship is presented, in which air travel is shown (graphically) to vary inversely with the cube of price. However, the relation only holds over a certain (unspecified) range, and no further elaboration is made for this part of the problem.

with incomes over $10,000 as an index of business concentration, the authors are also including a measure of the proportion of families likely to use air travel for pleasure purposes. The statistical results are interesting, although the methods of sampling may be questioned.[24]

[24] Hansen, *op. cit.*, pp. 27–28.

Appendix D

Data and Sources

THE LETTERS in parentheses indicate, in the notation of Chapter 4, Section 2, and Chapter 5, Section 1, the parameters for which these data are relevant.

1. Data for 1957: The Historical Model

Demands (weekly) ${}^{J}D^{K}$

FROM \ TO	New York	Chicago	Miami	Los Angeles	Washington	San Francisco	Detroit	Boston	Cleveland
New York		8,990	9,100	3,830	6,330	2,460	3,230	7,200	2,660
Chicago	6,860		2,900	1,880	1,550	700	2,570	1,040	1,530
Miami	9,820	3,210		240	1,020	110	1,570	1,190	1,170
Los Angeles	3,640	1,960	210		810	7,930	620	530	350
Washington	6,350	1,560	1,010	840		640	720	1,170	530
San Francisco	2,510	1,030	110	7,930	690		350	350	160
Detroit	3,210	2,480	1,390	550	670	270		380	1,240
Boston	7,050	1,070	1,050	560	1,110	340	380		410
Cleveland	2,620	1,450	980	370	490	170	1,250	430	

Sources: Compiled from data in U.S., Civil Aeronautics Board, *Origin-Destination Airline Passenger Survey* (Washington, D. C.: Air Transport Association — Airline Finance and Accounting Conference, 1958), Vols. 1–3, March 1–17, 1957; also Vols. 1–3, September 17–30, 1957.

Regional Demands

Where region 1 = New York, Washington, Boston, Philadelphia
2 = Chicago, Detroit, Cleveland, St. Louis
3 = Miami
4 = Los Angeles, San Francisco
5 = Seattle
6 = Dallas
7 = Atlanta

FROM \ TO	1	2	3	4	5	6	7
1		22,200	12,230	9,370	1,070	1,370	1,830
2	21,830		5,590	4,490	470	1,070	890
3	13,200	5,990		340	40	110	740
4	9,230	5,050	310		2,910	630	180
5	1,000	520	40	2,970		60	30
6	1,340	1,020	120	510	40		180
7	1,830	920	700	140	20	190	

Sources: Same as preceding.

Aircraft Types

DC-7C (includes DC-7, DC-7B, L-1049G, L-1649A)
DC-6B (includes DC-6, DC-4, L-049, L-749, L-1049)
Viscount 700
CV-340 (includes CV-240, CV-440, M-202, M-404, DC-3)

Block Speeds for Representative Aircraft ($^J b_h^K$)

Stage Length (miles):	100	200	300	400	500	1,000	1,500	2,000+
Load Factor:			all 60 per cent					
Aircraft:								
DC-7C			210		240	270	290	290
DC-6B			200		220	240	250	255
Viscount 700	170	200	230		250	270		
CV-340	140	170	180	190	200			

Sources: Compiled from data in *American Aviation*, April 21, 1958, p. 92. George P. Baker and Gayton E. Germane, *Case Problems in Transportation Management* (New York: McGraw-Hill Book Company, Inc., 1957), p. 22; International Civil Aviation Organization, *The Economic Implications of the Introduction into Service of Long-Range Jet Aircraft* (Montreal: International Civil Aviation Organization, 1958), pp. 59, 61; S. P. Sobotka and M. Wiesenfelder, "Projections of Flight Crew Employment by U.S. Scheduled Airlines, 1961 and 1965," *Journal of Air Law and Commerce*, XVII (Winter, 1960), 50.

Seating Capacities ($^J_r a_h^K$)

DC-7C	70
DC-6B	66
Viscount 700	44
CV-340	42

Sources: Compiled from figures in *American Aviation*, April 22, 1957, pp. 123–124.
Baker and Germane, *op. cit.*, p. 83.
International Civil Aviation Organization, *loc. cit.*

Ranges (miles)

DC-7C	4,600
DC-6B	3,000
Viscount 700	1,400
CV-340	600

Sources: From data in Gotch and Crawford, *Air Carrier Analyses*, Quarterly, 1957, Schedule 47.
International Civil Aviation Organization, *loc. cit.*

Costs

Total operating costs per airplane-mile, by stage lengths (in cents) ($^{J}c_{h}^{K}$)

	Miles								
	0–200	200–400	400–600	600–800	800–1,000	1,000–1,500	1,500—2,000	2,000–2,500	2,500+
DC-7C	249	146	126	118	112	108	104	102	104
DC-6B	121	79	72	68	65	64	62		
Viscount 700	82	59	54	53	52				
CV-340	91	66	61						

Sources: Compiled from data in Gotch and Crawford, *op. cit.*, Schedule 51.
Sobotka and Wiesenfelder, *loc. cit.*

Number of Aircraft Available (S_h)

DC-7C	245
DC-6B	392
Viscount 700	59
CV-340	432

Source: *Aviation Week*, April 21, 1958, pp. 97 ff.

Utilization (hours per day) (S_h)

DC-7C	9
DC-6B	9
Viscount 700	9
CV-340	8

Sources: Gotch and Crawford, *op. cit.*, Schedule 47.
Cf. also International Civil Aviation Organization, *loc. cit.*

2. Data for 1963: The Projective Model

Demands (weekly) ($^{J}D^{K}$)

FROM \ TO	New York	Chicago	Miami	Los Angeles	Washington	San Francisco	Detroit	Boston	Cleveland
New York		17,670	18,900	8,800	12,980	4,900	6,100	15,900	6,060
Chicago	14,890		5,480	4,140	2,860	1,500	2,980	2,680	2,610
Miami	14,480	5,640		660	1,770	310	3,030	3,390	2,630
Los Angeles	8,310	3,920	760		2,090	14,800	1,040	1,560	1,060
Washington	13,060	2,600	2,210	2,350		1,900	1,180	3,630	1,150
San Francisco	4,450	1,320	290	14,900	1,800		390	770	310
Detroit	5,700	4,250	3,170	1,410	1,200	480		860	1,050
Boston	16,050	2,530	3,100	1,650	3,470	890	750		910
Cleveland	6,480	2,660	2,600	1,160	1,100	350	1,030	930	

Sources: Compiled from data in U.S., Civil Aeronautics Board, *Origin-Destination Airline Passenger Survey* (Washington, D. C.: Air Transport Association — Airline Finance and Accounting Conference), for years 1954, 1955, 1956, 1957, 1958. Method of projection explained in Chapter 5, Section 2.

Aggregate Demands

FROM \ TO	1	2	3	4	5	6	7
1		45,300	28,400	22,800	2,400	3,120	3,530
2	45,600		11,900	10,200	9,200	1,890	2,090
3	26,100	12,100		1,010	80	240	1,590
4	21,100	9,570	1,050		5,690	1,690	290
5	2,230	690	150	6,340		40	80
6	3,760	2,020	390	1,530	80		330
7	4,140	1,870	1,700	350	80	250	

Sources: Same as preceding.

Aircraft Types

707 (including DC-8, CV-880)
720
Electra
Viscount (700 and 800)

Block Speeds for Representative Aircraft ($^J b_h^K$)

Stage Length (miles):	100	200	300	400	500	1,000	1,500	2,000+
Load Factor:			all 60 per cent					
Aircraft:								
707			288		351	420	450	470
720			300		365	433	460	490
Electra			244		282	318	333	
Viscount	170		230		250	280		

Sources: International Civil Aviation Organization, *loc. cit.*
Sobotka and Wiesenfelder, *loc. cit.*
R. Dixon Speas, *Technical Aspects of Air Transport Management* (New York: McGraw-Hill Book Company, Inc., 1955), p. 282.
Boeing Airplane Company documents and reports.

Seating Capacities ($^J_r a_h^K$)

707	136
720	115
Electra	75
Viscount	54

Sources: International Civil Aviation Organization, *loc. cit.*
Boeing Airplane Company documents and reports.

Ranges (miles)

707	5,000
720	3,600
Electra	2,500
Viscount	1,500

Sources: Same as preceding.

Costs

Total operating costs per airplane-mile (in cents) (${}^{J}c_{h}^{K}$)

707	250
720	156
Electra	124
Viscount	100

Sources: Based on 1959 experience reported in *Aviation Week*, May 2, 1960, p. 54.
Also various Boeing Airplane Company reports. Breakdown by segment lengths was not possible.

Number of Aircraft Available (S_h)

707	218
720	113
Electra	127
Viscount	60

Sources: Writer's estimate, based on material in *Aviation Week*, May 2, 1960, *passim.*
American Aviation, April 21, 1958, pp. 37, 51.
Material from a U.S. airplane manufacturer.

Utilization (hours per day) (S_h)

707	10
720	10
Electra	9
Viscount	9

Sources: International Civil Aviation Organization, *loc. cit.*
Sobotka and Wiesenfelder, *op. cit.*, p. 81.
Reports in various issues of *Aviation Week* and *American Aviation* throughout 1959 and 1960.
Boeing Airplane Company documents and reports.

Index